MANAGING GROUP PROCESS

Marvin R. Gottlieb

Westport, Connecticut
London

Library of Congress Cataloging-in-Publication Data

Gottlieb, Marvin R.
    Managing group process / Marvin R. Gottlieb.
        p.   cm.
    Includes bibliographical references and index.
    ISBN 1–56720–511–9 (alk. paper)
    1. Teams in the workplace.   2. Group facilitation.   3. Management.   I. Title.
    HD66.G6778   2003
    658.4'036—dc21   2002029877

British Library Cataloguing in Publication Data is available.

Library of Congress Catalog Card Number: 2002029877
ISBN: 1–56720–511–9

First published in 2003

Praeger Publishers, 88 Post Road West, Westport, CT 06881
An imprint of Greenwood Publishing Group, Inc.
www.praeger.com

Printed in the United States of America

The paper used in this book complies with the
Permanent Paper Standard issued by the National
Information Standards Organization (Z39.48–1984).

10 9 8 7 6 5 4 3 2 1

Contents

Figures and Tables

FIGURES

TABLES

Introduction

A man once made a feast. He invited many townsfolk. Among them was a man of great distinction. He was a scholar and a sage, but a very modest man who disliked being honored. The host wished to seat him at the head of the table, as was his due according to custom. Instead, the man chose a place among the poor at the foot of the table near the door. Now, when the host, who was an understanding man, saw him do this he seated his other distinguished guests near him, saying: "My masters, wherever this man sits is the head of the table."

It is not the place that honors the man, but the man that honors the place.[1]

Unless you've been living in a cave, it should be apparent that the management landscape has changed. Long-term objectives that used to be three to five years have shrunk to one year or less. Constant reorganization, incorporating both expansion and contraction, often at the same time, has caused dynamic changes in the workforce. Where it was once possible to hand out assignments and have a high degree of expectation that the tasks would be carried through to completion, today's manager is lucky if he or she can keep some of the critical members of the team in place for the duration of a project. Even more frustrating is how many times the project itself is rendered obsolete or irrelevant before completion.

These factors and many others are breeding a cynicism into the organizational environment that erodes productivity, stymies individual development, and threatens to bring many top-performing companies to their knees. At the center of this crazy quilt is the manager. Often starved for resources, and overstretched with responsibility, the manager becomes a reactive element in the process and is driven further toward a task orientation. Yet when managers are evaluated as being unsuccessful, it is because they lack a proactive or strategic focus. The model executives of our time are always at the top of the organization and are revered for bold decisions or strategic moves that they instigated—or at least took credit for. But these models have little or no bearing on what is happening in the trenches. There may be much for the generals to learn from the style and substance of former GE chairman Jack Welch as a manager, but there is little opportunity to apply Welch's strategies on the front lines of day-to-day management.

Aren't we sick to death yet of hearing how we are living in an environment of constant change? Forgetting, perhaps, that the observation was made by Karl Marx over a century ago that constant change was at the heart of the modern world and, by extension, capitalism.[2] Citing Peter Drucker's writing, Robert Eccles and Nitin Nohria, in their book *Beyond the Hype: Rediscovering the Essence of Management*, point out that "every generation of management discourse portrays the present as especially challenging, stereotypes the past, and then paints a vision of the future that is sharply contrasted with it. Every generation believes itself to be on the forefront of a new managerial frontier and posits the coming of a new organization that will revolutionize the way people work and interact."[3]

They go on to make the case that the only things that change about management are the words used to describe it. Today's "knowledge worker" appears in Drucker's writings of the 1950s; "autonomous management" became "commitment-based management," which morphed into "team-based management" and then "management by objectives (MBO)." Today's managers have become "professionals" and "leaders." The truth is that the underlying basics of management have not changed, if Drucker is to be believed, since 1920.[4] The role of the manager is still to get work done through others, to plan, organize, staff, control, and direct the work efforts of subordinates. In addition, the manager has to interact effectively with the total system, with other managers, and with superiors to create successful outputs for the organization. And it has always been so.

What this book proposes probably does not rise to the lofty heights of theory. The focus here is on practice. The requirements of management are the same, but the manager needs to approach the same objectives in a different way. The difference in approach is required because, as I said earlier, the landscape has changed. Faced with both the gifts and the challenges of technology, the demands for short-term financial gains, and an increasingly self-centered workforce, a successful manager will modify his or her approach to achieving the traditional managerial goals.

Too many managers are still stymied in their desire to take action because they are waiting for directions from above. Often these sought-after directions never come. Or if they do, they come too late in the day to be implemented effectively. In my role as an executive coach, I continually encounter highly motivated and talented managers who feel they cannot take action until they get clear direction and later are faulted for not having initiative. To be an excellent manager—and perhaps as important, to be recognized as such—is to strike a balance between commitment and risk. When I sit with managers complaining about their inability to take action, I ask them to give me three possible scenarios describing what the decisions or directions would be when and if they are ultimately passed down from the upper regions of the organization. Almost invariably these managers are able to outline three scenarios that are sometimes closely aligned with one another and other times widely divergent. In either case, the options of what could possibly be put forth are finite and illustrate that the manager fully understands the possibilities.

The second part of the exercise is for the manager to look at the three scenarios and, for each, to make a determination of how his or her specific department or function would be affected. Often the manager discovers that regardless of how divergent the potential scenario may be, the impacts and the resulting actions that must be taken are strikingly similar. Therefore, we conclude that many managers who are looking for direction are actually seeking permission. Of course, there are certain kinds of actions that require resources that cannot be undertaken until the dollars, personnel, or equipment are supplied. But I have long held that there are always significant actions that a manager can take that will positively impact the department's goals, or his or her status among direct reports, and contribute significantly to the success of the organization as a whole.

To do this, managers need to adopt a "hands-on" approach—not a hands-on approach to tasks but a hands-on approach to process. Command and control approaches do not work effectively under the current business circumstances, nor does simply walking around creating visibility and telling everyone they are doing a great job, although I support that as well. The most successful managers of today are those who perceive the need for facilitating, problem solving, decision making, and implementation of everything from communication channels to throughput on the factory floor. They develop the skills needed to work directly with their work groups and teams to create a true sense of partnership and responsibility.

This book is about managing group process. It asserts that in order to be effective, managers need an understanding of how groups function within organizations and how people can interact effectively within those groups. They need to involve themselves in hands-on facilitation of the key issues and processes that affect the success of their own organization as well as the broader community. They need the skills to create environments that enable people to function at their highest levels and bring a large measure of commitment to the work they do. While others have seen facilitation as a process separate from managing or leading, I see it as an integral part of management style. Facilitation is more than just a process; it is a mind-set or worldview that influences every aspect of managing.

The book is divided into three parts. Part I provides the reader with background in group process and the ways groups function within organizations. Part II shifts focus to the practicalities of working directly with groups in order to accomplish a variety of substantive as well as interpersonal objectives. Part III examines some tools that managers can use to lead groups toward clarity of issues, quality decision making, and strong individual commitment. All of the things presented here can be learned. And once learned, they can be applied to solving real-world management problems. Those managers who succeed in working with groups effectively will be highly valued by both the people who work with them and the organizations they serve. Of them it may be said: Wherever they sit is the head of the table.

NOTES

1. Nathan Ausubel, ed., *A Treasury of Jewish Folklore: Stories, Traditions, Legends, Humor, Wisdom and Folk Songs of the Jewish People* (New York: Crown, 1948), 58.

2. Karl Marx, *The Communist Manifesto*, in *The Marx-Engels Reader*, ed. Robert C. Tucker (New York: W.W. Norton, 1972), 476.

3. Robert G. Eccles and Nitin Nohria, *Beyond the Hype: Rediscovering the Essence of Management* (Boston: Harvard Business School Press, 1992), 25.

4. Peter F. Drucker, *People and Performance: The Best of Peter Drucker on Management* (London: Heinemann, 1977), 19.

PART I

Groups as a Challenge to Leadership

We begin with a basic understanding of groups as part of the organizational system. Chapter 1, "The Group as a System," looks at the factors that influence the dynamics of groups.

Chapter 2, "The Role of Groups in Today's Organizations," examines the way groups function to achieve the work of the organization. Work groups are distinguished from teams, and communication networks are examined.

Chapter 3, "Group Leadership Strategies," shows how working effectively with groups has become a key component of management success. Various leadership theories are examined as well as the role of "style."

Chapter 4, "Types of Meetings," begins to narrow our view of the type of group involvement a manager has. It points out that different types of meetings require adjustments in the facilitator's approach.

CHAPTER 1

The Group as a System

"... So, then he says, 'I don't think that is a good way to go,' and he storms out of the meeting!" The senior vice president sitting across from me (let's call him Doug) was fuming. He was part of a management team charged with the responsibility of consolidating some of the functional areas of the division. "Part of what burns me up is that he's the new guy. Ever since he got here these meetings have been a disaster. It didn't used to be that way. I mean, we all get along. All of a sudden we're at each other's throats over every issue."

"So what happened after he left?" I asked.

"Well, everyone looks at me as if to say, 'What are you going to do about this?' and I'm not the official chairman of this group."

This is a coaching session, so I am more concerned with Doug than the issue. I follow up, "What did you do?"

He pushed his chair back a little, showing discomfort. "I agreed to talk to him off line."

"Did you?"

"Yes, and it wasn't a great experience."

"What happened?"

"I followed him to his office and told him he was upsetting the group and asked him if there was something we could do to bring him more toward cooperation. He says, 'I'm not here to make friends.' I felt stupid just standing there, so I left."

Aside from the more specific problem of getting the tasks accomplished, Doug has described a classic example of what happens when a new person is introduced to an existing group—everything changes.

My wife and I look back with amusement at our discussions about how the arrival of our first child would not significantly alter our life-style. Nothing has ever been the same since. A whole new set of relationships had to be set up, in addition to the adjustments that had to be made in the existing relationships. In effect, the introduction of the new entity altered the "system," the relationships among interdependent components or forces. General systems theory provides a springboard for examining the way organizations work and, further, how subgroups within the organization interact.

OVERVIEW OF GENERAL SYSTEMS THEORY

General systems theory helps provide a framework for looking at complex human groupings like organizations, families, and other small groups. Groups are complex. Many individual elements affect the way a group operates: the reason the group was formed, the personalities of the members, the information or resources the group has, the type or style of leadership, how the group manages conflict or ambiguity, and what it will define as success. When applied to the organization, systems theory describes the organization as a complex set of interdependent parts that interact in ways intended to adapt to the constantly changing environment. An organization is described as made up of components consisting of individuals, structural and functional groups, technology, and other equipment. All of the system's parts are dependent upon one another in the performance of organizational activity, and any change in one part influences change in the other components.

Like all systems, organizations take in raw materials from the environment (*inputs*), process these raw materials (*throughputs*), and return something back to the environment (*outputs*). In the process of doing this, the organization's various parts interact in a variety of ways to convert the raw materials (could be pig iron, could be data) and produces outputs that are different from and greater than the raw material inputs. We say "greater than" because system processes are supposed to be *nonsummative*. That is, the interaction of the parts produces outputs that are greater than what they could produce individually. While I can't vouch for the truth or accuracy of this story, it helps make the point. My father-in-law worked most of his life with Raytheon. He used to tell a story about the early period of microwave transmission. It seems that a group of engineers were working on an experiment when an engineer from another division attended a demonstration. At some point, as my father-in-law tells it, the engineer approached the experiment, which was designed as a communications process, studied it for a while, and announced, "Yes, I can cook with it." Working at its best, the organization's parts act creatively in processing the different inputs to produce appropriate outputs to achieve organizational goals.

In discussing systems theory in the context of organizational communication, Gary Kreps underscores the importance of communication for achieving quality output. Discussing what he calls "equifinality," he says, "This indicates that organizations, through the interdependent efforts of their members, have the ability to perform many different activities to achieve a wide range of goals beginning from a variety of conditions by adapting the activities of its personnel and utilizing its organizational resources flexibly. Communication is the means by which organizations can adapt personnel and processes to the specific situations and problems they face."[1]

GROUP SYSTEMS IN CONTEXT WITH THE ORGANIZATION

Several of these systems theory principles are applicable to our examination of group process. For example, the concept of interdependence as demonstrated by Doug's scenario shows how the dynamics of a group can be radically changed by the introduction of a new member. However, it's not just the fact that there is a new member but also that the new member brought with him a set of values that were contrary to the group norms.

The nonsummative concept also relates to group process. In a horse race, we might look at the individual performance record of each horse to determine which one to bet on. However, if we applied the same principle to a football or basketball team, we could not explain how on some days teams with players who have inferior statistics rise to the occasion and turn in a winning performance over supposedly superior opponents. The group is producing an output that is greater than the sum of its parts—or positive synergy. One case in point is the 1980 U.S. Olympic men's hockey team. Clearly acknowledged by everyone to be the weaker team, they managed to beat the Russian team and make history. A great team that has a bad day may be suffering from negative synergy.

A few years ago, I was engaged to facilitate a software development project that required the commitment and active participation of the organization's development group, marketing group, sales group, administration, and quality control. When I met separately with the heads of each of these components, to a person they decried how it was impossible to accomplish the task within the specified time frame. When we all met together at an off-site location, I proposed a hypothetical exercise. I used butcher paper and posted on the wall a calendar that covered the full span of time between that day and the projected deadline for the project. I asked the group to approach the problem hypothetically. "Assume we actually met this deadline, what would have to be accomplished in what order and at what completion points in order to pull it off?"

I won't say they entered the process enthusiastically, but they were captured for the time being and took a stab at it. Working backwards from the target date, they set about to prove that it couldn't be done. What they began to discover was that it could be done. I remember the moment it started to happen. The head of Quality Control offered dismissively that he would have to have a particular component completed and in his hands by such and such a date in order to test it for release to the field. At which point the head of the development team said, "Well . . . I think we can do that." And so it went up the line. People began to discuss the possibilities, to think creatively, to make commitments. The group was energized, pulling together as a team.

One factor that came to light was that these people had never all been in one room at the same time. Also, their busy schedules made it difficult to meet, discuss, and coordinate their issues during regular business hours. We scheduled a follow-up session at the midstage of the project that involved having them all together again but with one innovation: we set up a schedule that allowed each individual to meet with his or her counterpart as needed for some period of time one on one during the off-site. Not only was the project a major success, but it was completed one month early!

Given the circumstances, the choice to use a professional facilitator was probably the right one. However, on reflection, there was nothing that we did that was so complex that a savvy manager with good facilitation skills couldn't have done. In fact, one of the key elements carried away from the project was the project planning methodology.

THE INFLUENCE OF FORCES BOTH OUTSIDE AND INSIDE THE GROUP

There are so many variables that influence whether a group will experience positive or negative synergy that it is hard to predict. Systems theory refers to this complex web of variables as "multiple causation" and warns against the oversimplification of how groups function. Some research points to the fact that a primary determinant for positive or negative synergy is the amount of ambiguity experienced by the group members. This suggests that the amount and quality of communication among group members play an important role in developing positive outcomes.[2] In this regard, it is a primary role of a facilitator or anyone with a need to manage group process to affect behaviors and establish environments that will promote the full exchange of information—about the subject at hand, about the people who are involved, and about the influences outside of the immediate group that will have some effect on the group's output.

These variables can be further classified as either "individual" or "system-level" variables.[3] Individual variables relate to the traits of the individuals involved in the group process: attitudes, values, beliefs, skills, experience, and any other factors unique to a particular individual that shapes behavior. At the system level we look for characteristics or norms of the group as a whole: organizational culture, group cohesiveness, procedures, and the structure and direction provided by anyone who would try to manage the group process.

In our opening scenario, the new person had both individual characteristics and a set of system-level values that were in direct conflict with the group norms. Part of the antagonism and hardening of position by the newcomer may be attributed to the ambiguity produced by this disconnect between his approach to group interaction brought from a very different corporate culture and the new culture he had entered.

As we discussed, *input* is the raw material the organization needs to transform. Other variables are related to the systems concept of *throughput*, how the group transfers inputs into final products. These variables include the various roles, rules, norms, and other procedures the group follows. Leadership also strongly influences throughput and the way group members communicate.

Output variables are the group products including tangible work completed such as reports, policies, changes in the way the organization operates, or actual products and services. These outputs generate *feedback*, which can come from the environment outside the organization as well as from within. Feedback between and among the components of the system allows the adjustment of processes according to the needs of the system as a whole. These feedback loops allow organization members to maintain a homeostatic balance of organizing processes. Organizational environment is more than the physical surroundings (buildings, offices, people, equipment) that organization members encounter. It is the information provided by the environment that makes them react. According to Karl Weik's model of organizations, the focus on environment shifts from a traditional structural, static view of physical surroundings to an action, process view of the messages that organization members perceive and the meanings that they create in response to these messages. The concept of organizational environment is embedded with communication. So whether the feedback is coming from inside or outside the organization, it is the communication dynamic that will determine whether or not the system responds negatively or positively to the stimulus.[4]

During the time this book was being prepared, the country was still reacting to the collapse of Enron and Tyco, and a host of other corporate debacles. The precollapse environment was created and sustained for a protracted period because communication was closely guarded and carefully managed by people both with and outside the organization. The communication structure was as faulty as the financial structure. Organizational systems are not immune to manipulation from within and without.

There is an attitude residing with some managers that the quality of a group's output is primarily within the group's control. As long as the group has the right people in terms of skill, knowledge and motivation, and effective leadership, so the argument goes, the group will produce high-quality outputs independent of, or in spite of, outside influences. Research into this notion seems to point in another direction. A study by Broome and Fulbright found that organizational factors beyond the group's control often had strong negative effects on performance.[5] Other studies have highlighted environmental factors as one of the three

Figure 1.1
Components of an Organizational System

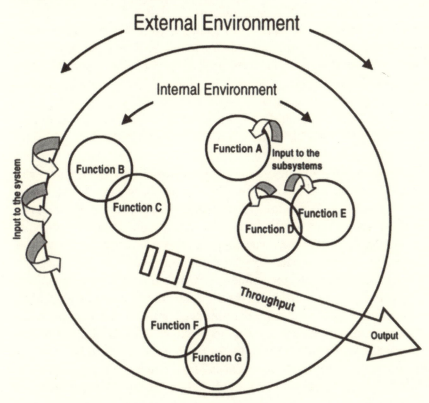

key factors that either helped or hindered the group's efforts. The other two were individual factors (such as skill and motivation) and leadership.

Figure 1.1 depicts the various components of an organizational system and illustrates how they interact. There is an external environment that influences the entire system by providing both raw material in the form of information and feedback on the effects of the organization's outputs. There is also an environment that is internal to the organization that provides input and feedback to the various subsystems (departments) in the organization.

The diagram suggests that there are some subsystems that interact closely or actually overlap in some ways. For example, many organizations have an overlapping association between Human Resources and

Training, Sales and Marketing, or Sales and Service. In other cases, a subsystem will not overlap with others; Finance comes to mind, as do Quality Control, Facilities, and Security.

A characteristic of successful organizations is that they have many individuals who function as *boundary spanners*, people who move freely between the internal and external environment as well as between the subsystems and bring feedback into the system from these environments. However, systems have degrees of openness to the outside environment. A public relations organization would keep a keen ear tuned to the changing world, while a group such as the Branch Dividians would vociferously shut it out.

Added to this mix are groups that are formed to act as boundary spanners within the organization. These "cross-functional teams," as they are often referred to, are designed to work as an independent subsystem to create outputs generated by specific objectives that fall outside the domain of any one subsystem. Cross-functional groups pose a special challenge to anyone who would manage them. They are particularly susceptible to the influence of the departments the members represent. How well cross-functional groups fare is often dependent on the quality of the relationship between the subsystems they come from.

One example comes from a large management consulting firm that has attempted to build a "faculty" of internal people to work with the training group to provide practical field experience and program facilitation. The effort is continually hobbled by the fact that the priorities are set outside the group. So if a person is scheduled to facilitate a program or attend a curriculum-building meeting and a client issue arises, that individual is yanked off the training assignment, often at the last moment. This leads to a scramble to find someone to fill in who may or may not be prepared to assume the role effectively.

Systems theory concepts help us avoid oversimplifying group dynamics. They point out that groups are constantly changing, so operational procedures or our general approach to managing groups cannot be fixed in place and then ignored. There are many reasons why groups succeed or fail. Systems theory invites us to look at multiple outcomes or effects for each individual action. If managers are going to become effective at managing group process, they have to consider all of the elements influencing the workings of the group and the way these elements interact.

CHARACTERISTICS OF SUCCESSFUL GROUPS

Since groups have a variety of purposes for forming within the organization, it is impossible to develop one model that would account for the characteristics of success for all. However, there are several characteristics that are common to most groups that deliver on their objectives.

1. All members understand the group's purpose and believe in the value of the objectives and the ability of other members to contribute meaningfully to the group product. In the best of circumstances the group will have a common goal. This common goal supercedes the many other goals present in the group. Individuals have goals that may be shared with others in the group, or they may be divergent and personal. One member may support a proposal because it favors a special interest he or she has, while another may be arguing for a different idea to demonstrate leadership potential. There could be others who are in the group because of the recognition or prestige it brings. Despite these personal motives, all of these members share the primary goal of achieving a group product that satisfies all of their needs. The perception of "groupness" is directly related to the degree that a primary goal is shared and acted upon among the members.

A group will be ineffective if the task and expected outcome are not clear. Charges for most group activity in organizations come from outside the group. Or charges may come from the group if the group is formed by some authority in the organization that perceives a problem. Rarely does the group get to pick its own topics for discussion. There was a recent commercial running on television—the product escapes me, so it probably wasn't as effective as it should have been from the advertiser's point of view—that showed a group of workers gathering around a conference table. They sat in silence for a few minutes, and finally one member asked, "Who called this meeting?" Everyone looked around at each other. No one took credit for calling the meeting, so it broke up. While not to this extreme, I have sat with groups that spent an extraordinary amount of time determining that they didn't know for sure what they were supposed to do.

Charging authorities are not always clear on their intent for the group; or worse, they alter their point of view before the group actually begins work based on other input from the environment in the interim.

A group without clear purpose or with disagreement among the members as to the goal will become disillusioned, confused, and paralyzed. Managing group process begins with a clarification of the group's purpose.

2. The group is small enough for the members to have general awareness of each other and large enough to contain a variety of knowledge, skills, and perceptions to develop a high-quality product. There are many factors that govern the size of various groups in the organization. However, when you do have control over how a group is constituted, it is good to know some of the thinking on limits of effectiveness. For example, research on problem-solving groups suggests the most efficient number is between five and seven. With less than five, a group lacks the diversity of input necessary for a broad perspective and consideration of various points of view. Members in a four-person group tend to be more reluctant to disagree. When the group exceeds seven members, there is a tendency for developing hierarchies and subgroups. If unequal status is ascribed to various group members, they will tend to dominate, while weaker members will develop esteem issues and may seek to undermine the group product by stimulating negative outside influence.[6]

3. There is a clear definition of the group's relationship to other parts of the organizational system. Effective groups have a high awareness of the boundaries of their charge. They know what to expect in the way of support from other groups in the organization. They locate and manage competitive forces in the environment that could affect group product. Members engage in boundary-spanning activities to ensure the constant flow of current information to the group, and they prepare for adaptation if something key to the process changes in the environment.

4. There is a clear definition of group members' relationships with one another. Members understand and accept their tasks and responsibilities toward the group product. They view each other as dependable, concerned, and committed. People show up on time for meetings, complete assignments in a timely manner, and make an effort to keep all group members informed of progress or problems on a regular and continuing basis. Group roles, whether assigned or assumed, are consistent with the knowledge or skill set of each individual. These roles are generally accepted by everyone and remain relatively stable throughout the process. The work of the group is shared equally (insofar as it is possible) so everyone feels that all are doing a fair share. Members feel secure enough with one another, regardless of assigned status, to exert influence on others and express contrary points of view.

5. *Everyone in the group abides by established norms.* While roles ascribe certain behaviors to individuals, norms are expectations for particular behaviors expected of the entire group. Common group norms would include:

- attending meetings
- showing up for meetings on time
- speaking in turn without interrupting others
- participating on a regular basis
- accepting and completing work assignments
- demonstrating enthusiasm for the group's work

Group norms are generally categorized in three ways: social norms, procedural norms, and task norms. Social norms provide standards and limitations that structure the relationships between individuals in the group. How honest will we be with each other? Can we express emotion? How much? Until a group refines its own norms toward social aspects of interaction, groups gravitate to the implicit established norms of the society and/or the organizational culture in which they reside. Procedural norms relate to how the group operates. Will majority rule? Or do we need a complete consensus? Will one person be in charge of managing the communication flow? Or will the discussion be more free form in nature? Task norms relate to how the group will approach the specific goals and objectives. Are we looking for the best possible solution? Will we compromise? Are we driven more by quality or expediency?

Some groups will develop norms that are specific to the group.

- They may elect to meet in one particular place.
- Time limits may be set for meetings.
- Members may be expected to respond in a particular order or follow other procedures.
- The group may wear uniforms.
- Members may adhere to a distinct vocabulary.

Specialized group norms emerge as the members spend time and interact with one another. There is a strong tendency for groups to develop some degree of uniqueness in their standards and expectations for certain behaviors on the part of group members. This helps the group differentiate members of the group from nonmembers. A group needs to have the means to distinguish itself from other groups in the environment. The establishment of norms helps accomplish this need for distinction.

6. Everyone receives personal satisfaction from participating in the group's activities and product. Personal satisfaction can come from an altruistic perspective, such as feeling good about the work the group is doing because it is perceived as inherently "good" for the organization or for society. Or it can come from career building, affiliation with a group that has status, or other recognition motives.

7. There is sufficient time to meet the objectives. While there are many ways to build efficiency into group process, many of which we will cover in more detail in later chapters, groups inherently take more time than individuals to solve a problem or make a decision. They need time to work through various procedures, to listen to and evaluate the input from all members, and to digest and process all of the available information. I have seen (and served on) countless committees and boards that were essentially "rubber stamps" for the solutions and decisions already arrived at by the chair or a few individuals. This happens, at least in part, because time constraints do not allow for a full and adequate airing of the issues, or the members are not willing to commit the volume of time necessary to work through a full group process.

8. A meeting place is regularly available that is conducive to group process. Few organizations, to my knowing, provide for adequate meeting space. This is particularly troublesome when you consider that estimates place the amount of time most people spend in meetings at 50 percent or above. I recently was sitting waiting for an appointment in the reception area in one of several buildings occupied by a financial media organization when five people carrying note pads and other materials came in and announced to the receptionist that they were in the middle of a meeting but had to leave their space because someone else had the room scheduled. They wanted to continue their meeting. The receptionist, who was in charge of scheduling conference space in that facility, checked the schedule for availability and informed the group that there was no place for them to go. I then watched while a member of the group called receptionists in two other facilities to request space available. There was none to be had. They left very dispirited. We could chalk this up as poor planning on their part in underestimating the amount of time they would need, except for the fact that I have witnessed this same scene countless times. I have on many occasions wandered from place to place with a group in search of a space, only to end up crammed into someone's small office or cubicle with knees touching and nowhere to put anything down.

THE LIFE SPAN OF A SYSTEM

Any entity established as a system has as one of its primary goals the survival and continuation of the system. The common life cycle in nature encompasses conception, birth, growth and development, maturity, decline, and death. Living organisms constantly adapt to changing environmental conditions in order to remain alive and healthy as long as possible. In the same way, human groups and organizations usually do anything in their power to ensure their own continuation. When a group is formed, a myriad of factors needs to be aligned before the group can be fully functional: The members have to learn each other's strengths and weaknesses, sort out each other's affiliations and loyalties, identify and accept leadership, set norms, and establish and commit to roles. Once this is done, the group can become productive. Individual members may leave or be replaced, but the group can continue functioning as long as its objectives are relevant to the larger organization. When a purpose no longer exists, or a competing group takes over its charge, the group will cease to exist.

To effectively manage group process, managers have to be sensitive to all aspects of the group system. This understanding will provide the necessary perspective to conduct proper diagnoses and interventions to ensure that the group succeeds. Often a manager underestimates his or her ability to influence events. Even subtle changes of group norms or venues or the insertion of key information can realign or regulate a group system. In this way, managers do not have to legislate change. It occurs naturally as the system readapts and as individuals adjust their roles, relationships, and the way they interact with the system.

NOTES

1. Gary L. Kreps, *Organizational Communication: Theory and Practice* (New York: Longman, 1986), 101.

2. Abran J. Salazar, "Understanding the Synergistic Effects of Communication in Small Groups: Making the Most Out of Group Member Abilities," *Small Group Research* 26 (May 1995): 169–199.

3. Randy Y. Hirokawa and Dierdre D. Johnston, "Toward a General Theory of Decision-making: Development of an Integrated Model," *Small Group Behavior* 20 (November 1989): 500–523.

4. Karl Weik, *The Social Psychology of Organizing*, 2nd ed. (Reading, MA: Addison-Wesley, 1979).

5. Benjamin J. Broome and Luann Fulbright, "A Multistage Influence Model of Barriers to Group Problem Solving: A Participant-Generated Agenda for Small Group Research," *Small Group Research* 26 (February 1995): 25–55.

6. Robert F. Bales and Edgar F. Borgatta, "Size of a Group as a Factor in the Interaction Profile," in *Small Groups: Studies in Social Interaction*, ed. Paul A. Hare, Edgar F. Borgatta, and Robert F. Bales (New York: Knopf, 1965).

CHAPTER 2

The Role of Groups in Today's Organizations

Let us begin at once to consider the group process. Perhaps the most familiar example of the evolving of a group idea is a committee meeting. The object of a committee meeting is first of all to create a common idea. I do not go to a committee meeting merely to give my own ideas. If that were all, I might write my fellow-members a letter. But neither do I go to learn other people's ideas. If that were all, I might ask each to write me a letter. I go to a committee meeting in order that all together we may create a group idea, an idea which will be better than any one of our ideas alone, moreover which will be better than all of our ideas added together. For this group idea will not be produced by any process of addition, but by the interpenetration of us all. This subtle psychic process by which the resulting idea shapes itself is the process we want to study.

—Mary Parker Follett, 1918[1]

It appears that each generation of managers feels obligated to invent "new" approaches to solving organizational problems. Most likely, these managers are rediscovering old ideas that have been dressed up in new clothes. Eccles and Nohria in their book *Beyond the Hype: Rediscovering the Essence of Management* point out that the differences between modern theories and practices and older ones lie in how they are named rather than in their substance. Pointing to the work of Follett as an example, they point out that she "called for an emphasis on 'cross-functioning'—on the replacement of 'vertical authority' with 'horizontal authority'—in order to promote the exchange of knowledge in organizations."[2] They go on to point out that even a casual reading of management literature for over 75 years shows that every age "discovers" these principles. They summarize, "From such a reading, one thing becomes especially clear: even as the fundamental themes of management remain the same, the words used to express them constantly portray them as new."[3]

It is in this light that we begin our discussion of teams and groups in organizations. Neither concept is either new or revolutionary. The notion of decentralizing command and control of the decision process has been practiced in various forms by companies since early in the past century. Granted, there has, until more recent times, been an emphasis on hierarchical organizational structures, but within those structures, groups and teams were always a part of the process.

It is also an important consideration that groups and teams are not necessarily the same thing, and they come in many varieties. Often managers seek to develop a "team" and end up with something quite different because there was no clear definition of what type of group interaction was necessary to complete the tasks.

TIME SPENT IN GROUPS

If we just look at managers as a subcategory of the organization and ask how much time they spend with groups, we see the significance of groups to the organization as a whole. Several studies have been done over the last 30 to 40 years that indicate the time spent in meetings is remarkably stable and remarkably large. While there are now many general studies of managerial behavior and several suggestions on time management strategies, empirical studies of how managers spend their time are relatively limited in number. Titus Oshagbemi, using an intensive literature search employing the facilities of the Institute for Scientific Information Social Sciences Database, found only a total number of 64 publications on the subject for the 13 years between 1993 and 1981.

A further study using the Social Sciences Citation Index (from the Institute for Scientific Information Social Sciences Database) on "managerial time" and "time management" as key words or words in the title yielded additional studies. However, many of the studies do not contain empirical data on how managers spend their time. Although there were many empirical studies generally, these studies did not contain reported comparable data on the use of managerial time—the time spent by managers on their activities, the time spent at their different work locations, the time spent alone or with groups of people, and so on.[4]

A summary of the average percentage working hours spent by selected managers on various activities reveals that managers spend about half of their total working hours in meetings. These could be periodical, prearranged, or emergency meetings between managers or between managers and nonmanagers, occurring within or outside organizational premises. The findings of the Oshagbemi study are shown in Tables 2.1 and 2.2.

A 1998 study of UK businesses commissioned by MCI WorldCom Conferencing and carried out by Research Business International finds the typical busy professional attends nearly 60 meetings a month, of which more than 10 percent involve travel out of town. A similar study—"Meetings in America: A Study of Trends, Costs and Attitudes toward Business Travel, Teleconferencing and Their Impact on Productivity"—by networkConferencing in the US, concurs, finding that the typical busy professional attends more than 60 meetings a month. If we assume that the meetings average one to two hours, the more recent studies seem to agree with the Oshagbemi study on the number of hours spent in meetings.

If there is a phenomenon more aligned with current organizations, it is that more unscheduled meetings are taking place. From the available studies, the percentage of working time spent in scheduled meetings was generally higher than the working time spent by managers in unscheduled meetings. However, the number of unscheduled meetings was usually higher than the number of scheduled meetings.

In some studies, such as those of Mintzberg and Kurke and Aldrich, there were remarkable differences between the percentage scheduled and unscheduled time spent in meetings. In Mintzberg's study, for example, 59 percent of total working time was spent in scheduled meetings, whereas only 10 percent was spent in unscheduled meetings.[5] These figures compare broadly with those of Kurke and Aldrich, which were 50 percent and 12 percent, respectively.[6]

In other reported studies, however, the differences between the time spent on scheduled and unscheduled meetings could be very small. For example, in Lawrence's study, the figures obtained were 22 percent and

Table 2.1
Details of Selected Studies on How Managers Allocate Their Time

Authors	Date	Sample
Copeman et al.	1963	58 managing directors in UK
Lujik	1963	25 chief executive officers in Holland
Brewer and Tomlinson	1963-64	six middle level managers in six UK firms
Hinrichs	1964	232 middle level managers in one U.S. company
Horne and Lupton	1965	66 middle level managers in ten UK firms
Thomason	1966	30 middle/low level managers in seven UK firms
Perkins et al.	1967	24 college presidents in 24 U.S. colleges
Mintzberg	1973	five chief executive officers in five U.S. firms
Cohen and March	1974	42 college presidents in 42 U.S. colleges
Pitner	1978	three superintendents
Kaplan	1979	six chief executive officers
Kurke and Aldrich	1979	four chief executive officers in four U.S. firms
Duignan	1980	eight superintendents
Willis	1980	three school principals
Snyder and Gluek	1980	two chief executive officers
Kmetz and Willower	1981	five school principals
Sproull	1981	five chief executive officers
Martin and Willower	1981	five school principals
Bussom et al.	1981	ten police chiefs
Morris et al.	1981	ten school principals
Larson et al.	1981	six superintendents
Oshagbemi	1988	26 heads of units in eight Nigerian universities
Oshagbemi	1988	12 heads of units in nine UK universities
Stewart	1988	160 senior and middle level managers in UK
Martinko and Gardner	1990	41 principals in 41 U.S. schools

Source: Titus Oshagbemi, "Management Development and Managers' Use of Their Time," *Journal of Management Development* 14.8 (1995): 7, table II.

20 percent.[7] Similarly, in Choran's research, a figure of 21 percent was obtained for scheduled meetings and 15 percent for the percentage time spent in unscheduled contacts.[8]

The discrepancies in these findings suggest that there are other determinants such as organizational culture or even the type of business. A law firm may have a preponderance of scheduled meetings, whereas

Table 2.2
Findings of Selected Studies of the Working Hours of Managers

Authors	Average Total Weekly Hours
Copeman et al., 1963	44
Lujik, 1963	60
Horne and Lupton, 1965	44
Mintzberg, 1973	40
Cohen and March, 1974	55
Kurke and Aldrich, 1979	44
Oshagbemi, 1988	43
Stewart, 1988	42

Source: Titus Oshagbemi, "Management Development and Managers' Use of Their Time," *Journal of Management Development* 14.8 (1995): 7, table III.

a team of programmers at a high-tech company may require frequent unplanned interactions.

WHAT IS A GROUP?

Work-related groups can be divided into *formal* and *informal* categories. The formal groups are established by the organization and usually carry a title, such as Purchasing, Accounts Receivable, Safety Committee, Diversity Task Force, and so on. Informal groups share the same group characteristics as formal groups. They have members, goals, and interaction and exist over time, but they are not described on the organizational chart. The group may have lunch together, play on the company team, car pool, or be a collection of people who have simply developed an affinity for one another for a variety of reasons— information gathering, networking, or social. Effectively managing group process requires consideration of both the formal and informal group structures in the organization. In many ways, the informal structures carry more essential information.

While we provided data on meeting time in previous paragraphs, we all know that not all group interaction takes place in meetings. We will cover meetings in detail later, but a meeting has some clear differentiators from other gatherings. It has an objective, an agenda, and a sequence of events. There are other groups that interact in a multitude of settings without any defined group objective or process.

The word *group* can be used to refer to any assembly of people. Marketers study demographic groups or birth cohorts; commuters are referred to as a group; artists of a particular period, subject, or technique are called a group. For the purposes of our discussion, a group is defined in narrower terms. I have always appreciated Beebe and Masterson's definition of a group for its directness, accessibility, and clarity: "We define small group communication as interaction among a small group of people who share a common purpose or goal, who feel a sense of belonging to the group, and who exert influence on one another."[9]

In this definition, a group consists of at least three people. Three people are required in order for the dynamics of group roles, norms, power, status, and leadership to come fully into play. At the outer limit a group can have as many as 20 people and still be considered a small group, although there is little agreement among scholars on this issue. There is agreement, however, on what happens if the group becomes too large. The result is less individual member interaction, and the larger the group, the less influence each individual has on the group as a whole. Also, beyond a certain level, subgroups tend to develop. Subgroups occur out of a felt need for members of the group to align themselves with others of like mind in order to increase the strength of their position. Another factor that underlies the formation of subgroups is frustration about gaining access to the floor to present a point of view.

The small group is a subsystem within the larger organization. As such, it is subject to the same forces as the larger system. The behavior of one group member affects all of the others. Influencing behavior carries beyond the face-to-face meeting. Individual members interact "off-line" in settings other than meeting rooms. There continues to be an increase in mediated settings like teleconferencing, faxing, e-mail, and Web meetings. The temptation to use these tools increasingly to manage group process is strong. Because of time constraints and scheduling difficulties, it is appealing to send out e-mails and ask for a response. However, not everyone treats e-mail the same way. I know one executive who claims to check his e-mail once a week without fail! If you are waiting for a response from him, you can wait a long time. Spamming and other general annoyance factors have made people somewhat wary of e-mail as a conduit. Also, there are security and eavesdropping issues, either real or imagined, that cause people to edit in ways they might not if they were participating face-to-face with a trusted group. Often the key to making a program or project work lies in the quality and character of the relationships the manager establishes between himself or herself and the group, as well as the relationships fostered between the members of the group. Relationship issues are better handled in person than in any other way.[10]

TEAMS AND WORK GROUPS

It is fundamental to managing group process to determine what kind of group is being managed. The word *team* has overwhelmed our consciousness of what constitutes a group. Not every group is a team, although many managers refer to all groups that way. Recently, a senior vice president in charge of a technology division met with his direct reports and requested that they look for ways to cut 10 percent from the next year's budget without adversely affecting performance quality. The direct reports, six in all, went back to their areas of responsibility and independently developed plans and contingencies to report back to the senior vice president. Is this a poor exercise? Probably not. Will the mission be accomplished? Maybe. Were these direct reports working as a team? Absolutely not.

Jon Katzenbach and Douglas Smith report that they interviewed more than 50 different teams in 30 organizations, ranging from corporate giants like Motorola and Hewlett-Packard to Operation Desert Storm and the Girl Scouts. In so doing, they arrived at some interesting findings about how teams do and do not work. They concluded that the values of teamwork are worth advocating, including, as they do, listening and responding constructively, giving others the benefit of the doubt, providing support, and recognizing the interests and achievements of others.[11]

They go on to point out that teamwork values are not exclusive to teams or enough to ensure good team performance. Because of the broadening of the definition, *team* has become the catchword for any group working together. In fact, teams in the true sense are not necessarily appropriate for all work done by groups. So anyone who seeks to manage group process must make a determination of what kind of construct is best for the problem at hand. Group constructs can be divided into three categories: work groups, teams, and hybrids that incorporate both. Each of these constructs have several distinct characteristics.

Work Groups

A working group product is the result of what the group members do as individuals. Consider our senior vice president and his direct reports. Assuming that all six members report their findings at the next meeting and some action is decided upon, they have completed a work group assignment. Work groups are necessary and prevalent in all organizations. At their best, they come together to share information, perspectives, and insights to move decision processes forward. While the intelligence gathered from these meetings is, to some degree, helpful for each member, the primary reason for the interaction is to facilitate a better decision on the part of one person, usually a superior. However, whatever the reason or the outcome, the focus is always on individual goals and accountabilities. Work group members don't take responsibility for results other than their own.[12]

One form of work group that requires some attention is the virtual work group, misnamed as "virtual team." Virtual work groups consist of people operating at different locations, connected electronically by one means or another. The rise of virtual work groups has tracked with the need to work in real time across the globe. They may be composed of full-time or part-time employees in various permutations. These might include distant group members working with local in-house workers, or telecommuters working in a variety of configurations.

While technology has provided enormous opportunities for organizations to recruit and utilize talent without the constraints of location, it also creates some serious management problems including the challenges presented by 24-hour workdays and different time zones. Some of the complexities and subtleties of managing these work groups will be discussed in Chapter 3, "Group Leadership Strategies." However, the challenge for the manager focuses on managing the potential for randomness, chaos, and ad hoc decision making by putting processes in place to make the groups efficient and effective.

It may help to note that virtual work groups are rarely completely virtual. There is generally some face-to-face meeting and, at the very least, conference calling where people have access to verbal interaction.

In these circumstances, some teaming is possible since issues can be worked on simultaneously by several members of the group during the meeting. The necessity to interact face-to-face increases with the interdependency of the group members.

Teams

Teams also depend on individual results. However, when a group is truly functioning as a team, the product is the result of a large measure of collective effort. In addition to each member's individual accountability, the group also has mutual accountability. Let's say our senior vice president presented the task differently than to the direct reports: "Listen people . . . we need to cut our budget next year by at least ten percent. I want you all to get together and hammer out some approaches that won't affect the quality of the overall operation. I expect you to work together on this and agree on any options you bring to me."

The resultant activity among the six direct reports will most likely include discussion, debate, collaboration, and compromise. Potentially, the result could be greater than the expectation (nonsummative) because the group takes on more of the characteristics of a system.

The following comparison table (Table 2.3) is adapted from one provided by Katzenbach and Smith.[13] The table illustrates some of the key differences between work groups and teams.

Hybrids

It is almost inevitable that both work groups and teams will overlap in terms of the type of interaction they have. There will be times when teams will break from the collective and delegate various tasks and responsibilities to individual members. In the same manner, work group members may engage each other in dialogue to clarify an issue or argue a point. They may also engage in group decision-making activity that reflects the characteristics of team behavior. This type of hybrid activity takes place naturally; however, it can be applied effectively for managing group process. Certain tasks lend themselves to work groups and others lend themselves to team behavior. A skillful facilitator will manage the interaction of the group according to the needs of the problem or issue at hand.

In my teaching of group dynamics in both the university and private

Table 2.3
Key Differences between Work Groups and Teams

Work Group	Team
• Leadership is centralized with one person.	• Leadership is potentially shared among members.
• Each individual is accountable for his/her own actions.	• There is collective accountability.
• The group's purpose is set in response to organizational directives.	• The group's purpose is set in response to both organizational directives and a shared group mission.
• The group produces individual work products.	• The group produces one collective work product.
• Meetings focus on running efficiently.	• Meetings incorporate discussion, debate, and other active problem-solving interactions.
• The group measures its effectiveness by individually meeting the stated objectives.	• The group measures its effectiveness by collectively meeting the stated objectives.
• The group discusses and clarifies issues and objectives and then each member works individually.	• The group does the majority of the work together.

Source: Adapted from Jon R. Katzenbach and Douglas K. Smith, "The Discipline of
   Teams," *Harvard Business Review* (March–April 1993): 113.

sector during the last 30 years, I have consistently used one simple
exercise to make three points about groups:

1. People resist subsuming their individual effort in favor of the group.[14]
2. Given certain kinds of tasks, a team orientation will outperform a work
   group orientation.
3. All other things being equal, a group will always outperform an individual
   attempting the same task.

I call it "the Anagram Exercise." The exercise consists of dividing a
larger group (say, 20) into smaller groups (say, four groups of 5). The
groups are told that this is a competition. They are then given a word
(I use the word *BOOMERANG*) and asked to make as many words as
possible from the letters in the word within a 15-minute time limit. The

only stipulation is that the group must have all of their words on one list.

People resist subsuming their individual effort in favor of the group. Interestingly, the vast majority of groups will spend a fairly significant amount of their total time devising a scheme for accomplishing the task. For example, one group may decide to divide up the letters among the group members; another, to spend a certain amount of time working independently. The most common result is that a great deal of time is spent in the group situation working alone. The task is usually completed with a scramble at the end, with groups trying to reconcile their separate lists into one. My repeated observation of this pattern of behavior has convinced me that when left to their own devices, most people prefer to carve out some portion of the total work effort, separate themselves from the group, and work alone.

Given certain kinds of tasks, a team orientation will outperform a work group orientation. Although not empirically arrived at, I estimate that 20 percent of the total groups given this task approach it as a team. That is, they begin immediately working with one list and build it by working together. These groups invariably win the competition. They are more efficient by having eliminated the organization and consolidation steps, and they have the benefit of the extra stimulation or "synergy" that comes from hearing others generate words. The work groups tend to produce 40 to 50 words, while the teams achieve 50 to 60. I had one team produce 93 verifiable words.

All other things being equal, a group will always outperform an individual attempting the same task. I have administered the same challenge to individuals working on their own. These scores usually range between 35 and 45. One person, a senior professor of English, achieved a 55. This belies the notion that groups are more of a hindrance than a help—recall the joke about the camel being a horse designed by a committee. Groups should perform well. If they don't, it's not because there is something inherently wrong with the way groups work; it is because they haven't been managed effectively.

TYPES OF TASKS

The task outlined in the Anagram Exercise is highly *quantitative*; that is, I am asking the groups to produce a quantity of something, in this case, words. Other group tasks can be highly *qualitative*, meaning

Figure 2.1
Conflict Diagram

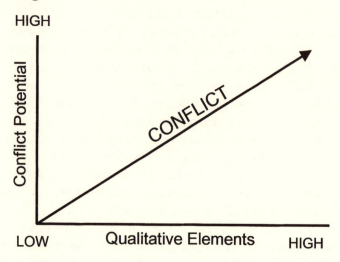

there is a lot of opportunity for attitudes, values, and beliefs to enter into the discussion. For example, if I ask a group to develop recommendations for a company dress code, there could be a number of points of view on the subject, and individuals might have strong feelings one way or another. The potential for emotion correlates with the potential for conflict in interaction. As Figure 2.1 suggests, as tasks become more qualitative, the potential for conflict increases.

Research into group conflict has pointed out that groups can work through conflicts successfully, and when they do, it strengthens the group's ability to deal with future conflicts.[15] In other cases, conflicts undermine the group process and set the stage for ongoing problems and reduced group effectiveness in the future.[16] Some recent research by Kuhn and Poole examines the longer-term effects of conflict on group performance. The study also considers what they call "task complexity" as a moderating variable, which aligns with the notion of quantitative and qualitative balance in relation to conflict.[17] The study classifies conflict management style into three categories: avoidance, distributive, and integrative.

Most group tasks contain some qualitative elements. The degree to which groups are able to manage the resulting potential for conflict will largely determine how effectively they perform. Note that I said "manage" conflict, not eliminate it. There is a tendency in organizational group process for people to withhold their true feelings or opinions for a variety of reasons, some political, others simply to avoid committing to additional work or responsibility.

GROUP COMMUNICATION NETWORKS

Left to their own devices, groups will develop communication patterns randomly. Simply put, a communication network is a pattern of message flow from one person to another and to the group as a whole. Patterns develop at the same time and along the same lines as norms and roles. They are influenced by member status, group size, individual expertise, the way the chairs are placed in a room, and many other factors. If the "boss" called the meeting, she may call on people individually. Soon people will not speak unless they have been called upon to do so. If Sam speaks frequently and comments on the interjections of others, the group will begin looking at Sam and expecting a comment each time someone speaks. Members who speak infrequently will find themselves increasingly ignored.

Visualize the group meetings in which you participate. You probably have a sense that most of the comments are addressed to the group as a whole. In fact, just the opposite is true. Relatively few comments are addressed to the group as a whole. Most interaction flows directly from one group member directly to other group members, often quite repetitively. These patterns may be established early or emerge over time, but they are remarkably stable. Once these patterns are established, they remain in place until something major changes in the group.

Types of Group Communication Networks

While many types of communication networks have been identified, there are two primary types that produce hybrids that account for the others.

The Wheel

Wheel groups take their name from the wheel and hub configuration such as a bicycle wheel. As indicated in Figure 2.2, in a wheel configuration, group members address their comments to one central person, who may be the designated leader, chairperson, or boss, depending on

Figure 2.2
Wheel and Free Form (Star) Configurations

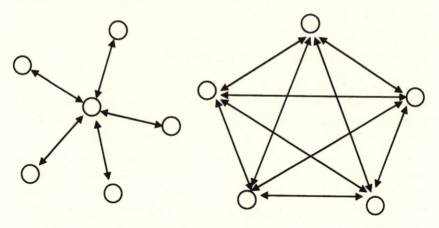

the setting. In this manner, the communication flow is restricted between the participants, providing for more efficiency than more open
patterns. The wheel group is the most common type of formal group
configuration. Most organizational meetings are called by someone—
boss or chair—who then presides over the process by directing questions and responses to group members individually and serially. Staff
meetings, board meetings, and committees all tend to fall into this pattern.

Because of the strong centralized communication pattern, wheel
groups move more quickly toward stated objectives. The inherent efficiency enhances group cohesiveness. The central person in a wheel
group is generally more satisfied with the communication pattern and
results than the other members. He or she can, however, suffer from
information overload and have difficulty making judgments or arriving
at a solution.

Free Form (Star)

In the free form or star configuration the group operates with a pattern that allows communication to take place between all of the members one to one or from one to the group as a whole. The effect is to
enable rapid communication among all members without having to get
clearance from a central gatekeeper. There is evidence to suggest that

Table 2.4
Advantages and Disadvantages of Wheel and Free Form Groups

Wheel Group		Free Form Group	
Advantages	Disadvantages	Advantages	Disadvantages
Judgments are arrived at quickly.	Leader can dominate outcome.	Judgments are generally more accurate.	It requires a longer time to move through the process.
Conflict is minimized.	Latent conflicts are not surfaced and resolved.	There is opportunity to resolve conflicts and build relationships.	Conflict can inhibit arriving at a judgment.
Everyone can be required to participate.	Participation is limited by the leader's questions.	Everyone can participate to the extent of their knowledge and interest.	A minority may dominate the input and outcome.
Groups can be kept focused on the topic or issue.	There is limited opportunity to discover "creative" alternatives.	Important related topics and issues get a hearing.	Group can lose focus and get off track.
Time limits can be enforced.	All issues and suggestions may not surface.	Groups have a full range of data on which to base judgments.	Inefficiency may cause members to lose interest.

free form groups tend to be more accurate in their judgments and more creative in their solutions to problems. Members of free form groups tend to be more satisfied with the outcomes, probably because they feel they have had a good opportunity to participate and present their views.

On the other hand, free form groups have a tendency to be inefficient. They will normally take longer to reach a decision. There is also more opportunity for the group to be bogged down with conflict or personal agendas.

Table 2.4 illustrates the positives and negatives for the two primary communication networks. Since both types of groups have advantages and potentially serious disadvantages, it points to the need for managing groups in such a way that the advantages are enhanced, while disadvantages are minimized or controlled. The ability to manage group process effectively begins with an assessment of what configuration will best meet the needs of the task or problem at hand. If, for example, there is an impending natural disaster such as a hurricane or severe energy crisis, the mayor of the threatened city will most probably and correctly call together all of the heads of the city's essential services including police, fire, health, and transportation and conduct a highly structured wheel-type meeting. Under these circumstances each participant has specific defined responsibilities that must be carried out in order to meet the threat effectively. While we can assume there is always something to be gained from the interaction and cooperation among these groups, because of the time-sensitive nature of the problem, it would be inappropriate to open up a free form discussion on disaster response processes or energy policies. On the other hand, after the hurricane has passed and the brown-outs have momentarily ceased, the same panel may be convened in a more free form manner to discuss and make judgments concerning future disaster response and energy policies.

In most work situations the need for one type of group configuration or another can alternate rapidly, depending on the situation. A free form group session may conclude with the assignment of specific tasks and responsibilities to individual members of the group, who at a subsequent meeting report back to the group in wheel fashion. Managers who would control group process need to take the time to think through what style of interaction will work best for each situation that requires group participation. By establishing a point of view and stating the configuration that he or she would like employed during the group process, a manager exerts a great deal of influence on both the internal dynamics of the subsequent meeting and the quality and character of the outcome.

This chapter began with the notion that groups have been with us for a very long time, that people in organizational life have been spending a great deal of their working time meeting in groups. It also appears that the escalating complexity of doing business in today's world will only increase the necessity for well-formed and well-functioning groups. We also need to focus on the fact that all groups are not necessarily teams, nor do all tasks require a team orientation for successful outcome. A key factor that determines the nature of group dynamics is the communication network that exists within any given group. Regardless of how they are configured, the underlying assumption is that when they are well managed, effectively running groups will produce far more satisfactory results than an individual working on the same task.

The manager's role is to make choices regarding the types of group configurations he or she wants employed for particular problems or issues. Managers also have the responsibility to establish and maintain the climate of the groups that work in his or her department. When opportunities are provided for free and open discussion, people tend to feel more personal satisfaction and are generally more productive. Managers who succeed in creating trusting, open exchanges between people and a high level of cohesiveness among members can keep disagreement and conflict in perspective.

The more cohesive a group is, the stronger its social bonds to tolerate conflict. Through the application of clear direction, consistency, and other leadership qualities, managers create a social reality within which their groups can function. Under the best of circumstances, this social reality gives people the freedom to assert their individuality within a predictable context. In short, they enter into potentially difficult situations with the knowledge that they are already accepted by the group. This social reality also determines the degree to which individual group members will take on the group's goals as their own.

Managing group process requires creating a climate that develops a degree of dependence on the group. This dependency on the group enables members of the group to influence one another more effectively. The combination of personal commitment to the group's goals, dependence on the group, and the group's power over individuals in the group is what produces positive group climate. Under these conditions, groups work harder than those groups with little cohesiveness. And with few exceptions, not only do individuals perceive greater satisfaction, but the groups themselves are more productive.

NOTES

1. Mary Parker Follett, *The New State* (New York: Longman, Green & Co., 1918). From Chapter II, "The Group Process: The Collective Idea." Available online at http://sunsite.utk.edu/FINS/Mary_Parker_Follett/Fins-MPF-01.html.

2. Robert G. Eccles and Nitin Nohria, *Beyond the Hype: Rediscovering the Essence of Management* (Boston: Harvard University Press, 1992), 5.

3. Ibid.

4. Titus Oshagbemi, "Management Development and Managers' Use of Their Time," *Journal of Management Development* 14.8 (1995): 7.

5. Henry Mintzberg, *The Nature of Managerial Work* (New York: Harper & Row, 1973).

6. L.B. Kurke and H.E. Aldrich, "Mintzberg Was Right! A Replication and Extension of the Nature of Managerial Work," *Management Science* 29.8 (1979): 975–984.

7. Peter Lawrence, *Management in Action* (London: Routledge and Kegan Paul, 1984).

8. I. Choran, "The Manager of a Small Company" (Master's thesis, McGill University, Montreal, 1976), referenced in Morgan W. McCall and Michael M. Lombardo, "Looking Glass Inc.: The First Three Years," *Technical Report* 13 (Greensboro, NC: Center for Creative Leadership, 1979).

9. Steven A. Beebe and John T. Masterson, *Communicating in Small Groups: Principles and Practices*, 5th ed. (New York: Longman, 1997), 6.

10. P.L. McLeod and J.K. Liker, "Electronic Meeting Systems: Evidence from a Low Structure Environment," *Information Systems Research* 3 (1992): 195–223.

11. Jon R. Katzenbach and Douglas K. Smith, "The Discipline of Teams," *Harvard Business Review* (March–April 1993): 111–120.

12. Ibid., 112.

13. Ibid., 113.

14. This observation primarily comes from a Western cultural orientation. Some Asian cultural norms encourage subsuming individual achievement to the will of the group.

15. K.A. Jehn, "A Multimethod Examination of the Benefits and Determinants of Intragroup Conflict," *Administrative Science Quarterly* 40 (1995): 256–282; L.H. Pelled, K.M. Eisenhardt, and K.R. Xin, "Exploring the Black Box: An Analysis of Work Group Diversity, Conflict, and Performance," *Administrative Science Quarterly* 44 (1999): 1–28.

16. Joseph P. Folger, Marshall Scott Poole, and Randall K. Stutman, *Working Through Conflict: Strategies for Relationships, Groups, and Organizations*, 3rd ed. (New York: HarperCollins, 1997).

17. T. Kuhn and M.S. Poole, "Do Conflict Management Styles Affect Group Decision Making? Evidence from a Longitudinal Field Study," *Human Communication Research* 4 (October 2000): 558–590.

CHAPTER 3

Group Leadership Strategies

Leadership is perhaps the most discussed and written-about subject in the entire spectrum of management deliberation, yet it continues to be the most elusive element to define. Part of the problem with trying to find out what leadership is by studying current tracts is that leadership is often described after the fact. The most common practice of defining leadership is to single out certain individuals in corporate or public life who by virtue of the fortunes of their companies in the marketplace, or the results of other actions in the world, as well as their own capabilities, acquire a patina we call "leadership." There is nothing inherently wrong with examining and taking inspiration from individuals who have met with success in any arena. However, in the final analysis, these examinations lead us to conflicting conclusions about the nature of leadership. Dr. Martin Luther King, Jr. would probably not have enjoyed the same success as the chief executive officer (CEO) of General Electric. By the same logic, Jack Welsh would probably not be world renowned for leading the civil rights movement.

For the most part the quality and character of leadership are inextricably tied to the group or entity being led. Though difficult to define, elements of leadership need to be discovered, internalized, and practiced by anyone who would aspire to managing groups of any size. Although at any moment shifting contingencies may require different types of leadership, there are perhaps three things about leadership that are universal.

UNIVERSAL CHARACTERISTICS OF LEADERSHIP

There Is a Felt Need for Leadership

In most situations where human beings congregate, there is a felt need for leadership. This need for leadership can be seen throughout the full range of reasons that groups form. Informal social groups require leadership in many of the same ways as groups that are formed to combat some real or perceived threat. Fashion leaders tell us what to wear; opinion leaders tell us what to think.

Leadership Is Emergent

Put any group of people together and give them a task, and within a relatively short period of time, they will naturally divide themselves into roles, and one of those roles will be leadership. Leadership emergence has been associated with a number of different characteristics. Some research points to the fact that emergent leaders usually are selected by elimination during a two-stage process. At first all members have potential to become the group's primary leader. However, during the first stage, those members who appear quiet, uninformed, or dogmatic are rejected by the others. In the second stage, people who try to lead in an authoritarian or manipulative manner are eliminated. Finally, the person most skilled in verbalizing ideas emerges as the leader by the consensus of the group.[1]

Other recent studies of leadership have pointed to other characteristics that are associated with leadership emergence. One of these is termed *self-monitoring*, which refers to a person's abilities to monitor both social cues and his or her own actions in a given situation. High self-monitors are sensitive to contextual cues, are socially perceptive, and are able to respond flexibly according to what seems needed at any given time.

Leadership Is Stable

A third factor about leadership is stability. Once a leader has been identified, groups are very reluctant to make leadership changes, even when they have determined that the leadership is less than optimal. These factors may seem at times to be in conflict with the ever-changing dynamics of the organization. However, if a designated leader has been in place for any significant period of time, the organization has made adjustments to compensate for the lack of leadership competency. In fact, others in the organization who feel empowered by filling a leadership vacuum will be threatened by the advent of new leadership.

The overall system of the organization and the subsystems are continually under pressure from the environment to adopt modes of communication that allow the individual units to quickly disseminate and receive information to make the most informed decisions. Leadership plays a significant role in how information flows in the organization. Strong stable leadership requires an understanding of both the formal and informal communication channels in the organization and the ability to apply techniques and strategies for influencing that communication.

LEADERSHIP IN CONTEXT

In Chapter 1 we looked at some of the characteristics of effectively functioning groups. One of those characteristics that stands out is a clear definition of group members' relationships with one another. Or to put it another way, the roles that each member plays in the process of working through the tasks the group has been assigned. The concept of leadership carries with it a mystique that tends to obscure the more earthbound fact that it is one of many group roles that can be played by several individuals, depending on the needs of the group at any given time. It is useful to identify the various roles that occur in group activity. Several approaches to role classification have been attempted and put forth over the last half century. However, the most enduring and widely accepted classification is the one developed by Kenneth Benne and Paul Sheats.[2] Despite the fact that their classification of roles was originally published in 1948, the Benne and Sheats classification is still widely accepted and used in the textbooks on group communication. In fact, more recent studies verify the current usefulness of this classification model.

The model breaks group roles into three types: task roles, maintenance roles, and dysfunctional roles. Understanding that all classification systems may oversimplify the situation by asserting that individuals will adhere to one role or another during the group interaction process, the model is useful in identifying what the specific role behaviors are. During the course of any group interaction various individuals may take on different role behaviors. However, when this is looked at in detail, we usually discover that despite the variances most people tend toward prevailing roles based on the context within which they are a participant.

Task Roles

Task roles relate to the task output of the group. They focus on the business of moving the action forward toward a conclusion, a decision, or a solution. See Table 3.1.

Social/Maintenance Roles

Maintenance roles affect the interpersonal dynamics of the group. They have a strong influence on social climate. See Table 3.2.

Dysfunctional Roles

Dysfunctional roles refer to those behaviors that are primarily self-centered and impede the progress of the group. See Table 3.3.

THE LEADER'S ROLE

One of the things that I have always found intriguing about this taxonomy is that the role of leader is not listed in any of the categories. That omission says more about what leadership is than had it been included as a category on its own. Leadership behaviors incorporate several of the roles listed as task roles, at least a few of the social and maintenance roles, and none of the dysfunctional roles.

For example, one might expect a leader to be an initiator, an information seeker, and in some cases, an information giver. Certainly, leaders seek and give opinions and take on a clarifying and coordinating role. Good leaders also energize their groups and provide evaluation and criticism of the group product. The primary social and maintenance roles that a leader might take on include being a supporter and encourager, a harmonizer when it is called for, and a gatekeeper to make sure that the groups are not stymied in their efforts to accomplish their tasks. When we attempt to articulate the role of the leader, we can see that it incorporates the potential for many different behaviors. The most successful leaders are those that have the span of understanding and the flexibility to move between various role behaviors as the need for them becomes recognized.

Executive leadership poses an additional challenge. Top managers need to function as leaders while they are facilitating activities with their direct reports. However, beyond the task of conducting or facilitating effective meetings with other executives and managers, those who would aspire to be recognized as organizational leaders need to project some qualities beyond simple role assimilation. These qualities can be grouped in three categories that I call the three Cs: consistency, commitment, and courage.

ORGANIZATIONAL LEADERS ARE CONSISTENT

Being consistent is not just a matter of doing the same things over and over. Consistency begins with developing a common vision that organizational members can understand and adhere to. It is a point of view about what the organization does and the manner in which business is conducted that underlies and influences all of the activities of organizational members. A climate of consistency provides clear direction and priorities, clarifies roles and responsibilities, responds to a set of core values that relate to all aspects of doing business, and remains relatively stable regardless of other changes occurring in the organizational system.

By and large, people tend to follow those that operate with a vision of where they are going. This vision must be accessible and appear unshakable. Some leaders generate this vision from within and then disseminate it to the people around them. Others work with their people to create a common vision. Regardless of how the vision is acquired, its presence will focus the direction and align the energy and resources of the organization to achieve the desired goals.

Successful managers tie their personal vision with the vision of the larger organization. They work with their direct reports to identify the mission and goals of each team, out of which come the roles and responsibilities of each individual.

Table 3.1
Task Roles

Roles	Typical Behaviors	Examples
1. Initiator/contributor	Contributes ideas and suggestions; proposes solutions and decisions; proposes new ideas or states old ones in a novel fashion.	*"How about taking a different approach to this chore? Suppose we . . ."*
2. Information seeker	Asks for clarification of comments in terms of their factual adequacy; asks for information or facts relevant to the problem; suggests information is needed before making decisions.	*"Do you think the others will go for this?"* *"How much would the plan cost?"* *"Does anyone know if those dates are available?"*
3. Information giver	Offers facts or generalizations that may relate to the group's task.	*"I bet Chris would know the answer to that."* *"Newsweek ran an article on that a couple of months ago. It said . . ."*
4. Opinion seeker	Asks for clarification of opinions expressed by other members of the group and asks how people in the group feel.	*"Does anyone else have an idea on this?"* *"That's an interesting idea, Ruth. How long would it take to get started?"*
5. Opinion giver	States beliefs or opinions having to do with suggestions made; indicates what the group's attitude should be.	*"I think we ought to go with the second plan. It fits the conditions we face in the Concord plant best . . ."*
6. Elaborator/clarifier	Elaborates ideas and other contributions; offers rationales for suggestions; tries to deduce how an idea or suggestion would work if adopted by the group.	*"If we followed Lee's suggestion, each of us would need to make three calls."* *"Let's see . . . at 35 cents per brochure the total cost would be $525."*

Role	Description	Example
7. Coordinator	Clarifies the relationships among information, opinions, and ideas or suggests an integration of the information, opinions, and ideas of subgroups.	"Sam, you seem most concerned with potential problems. Maria sounds confident that they can all be solved. Why don't you list the problems one at a time, Sam, and Maria can respond to each one."
8. Diagnostician	Indicates what the problems are.	"But you're missing the main thing, I think. The problem is that we can't afford . . ."
9. Orienter/summarizer	Summarizes what has taken place; points out departures from agreed-upon goals; tries to bring the group back to the central issues; raises questions about the direction in which the group is heading.	"Let's take stock of where we are. Rita and Anthony take the position that we should act now. Bill says, 'Wait.' Rusty isn't sure. Can we set that aside for a moment and come back to it after we . . ."
10. Energizer	Prods the group to action.	"Come on, guys. We've been wasting time. Let's get down to business."
11. Procedure developer	Handles routine tasks such as seating arrangements, obtaining equipment, and handing out pertinent papers.	"I'll volunteer to see that the forms are printed and distributed." "I'd be happy to check on which of those dates are free."
12. Secretary	Keeps notes on the group's progress.	"Just for the record, I'll put these decisions in a memo and get copies to everyone in the group."
13. Evaluator/critic	Constructively analyzes group's accomplishments according to some set of standards; checks to see that consensus has been reached.	"Look, we said we only had two weeks, and this proposal will take at least three. Does that mean that it's out of the running, or do we need to change our original guidelines?"

Table 3.2
Social/Maintenance Roles

Roles	Typical Behaviors	Examples
1. Supporter/ encourager	Praises, agrees with, and accepts the contributions of others; offers warmth, solidarity, and recognition.	"I really like that idea, Taylor." "Ada's suggestion sounds good to me. Could we discuss it further?"
2. Harmonizer	Reconciles disagreements; mediates differences; reduces tensions by giving group members a chance to explore their differences.	"I don't think you two are as far apart as you think. Henry, are you saying ____? Benson, you seem to be saying ____. Is that what you mean?"
3. Tension reliever	Uses humor or other means to reduce the formality of the situation; relaxes the group members.	"Let's take a break . . . maybe have a drink." "You're a tough cookie, Bob. I'm glad you're on our side!"
4. Conciliator	Offers new options when his or her own ideas are involved in a conflict; disciplines himself or herself to admit his or her errors so as to maintain group cohesion.	"Looks like our solution is halfway between you and me, Jeff. Can we look at the middle ground?"
5. Gatekeeper	Keeps communication channels open; encourages and facilitates interaction from those members who are usually silent.	"Meredith, you haven't said anything about this yet. I know you've been studying the problem. What do you think about ____?"
6. Feeling expresser	Makes explicit the feelings, moods, and relationships in the group; shares own feelings with others.	"I'm really glad we cleared things up today." "I'm just about worn out. Could we call it a day and start fresh tomorrow?"
7. Follower	Goes along with the movement of the group passively, accepting the ideas of others; sometimes serves as an audience.	"I agree. Yes, I see what you mean. If that's what the group wants to do, I'll go along . . ."

Building Vision and Mission

The best way of building a foundation for managing the group process in the organization is to engage in a visioning exercise. A vision in this sense is a statement of how the company or your department, or both, will look in the future. Each part of the organization should have its own vision of how it will contribute to the overall vision of the organization.

Table 3.3
Dysfunctional Roles

Roles	Typical Behaviors	Examples
1. Blocker	Interferes with progress by rejecting ideas or taking a negative stand on any and all issues; refuses to cooperate.	"Wait a minute! That's not right! That idea is absurd." "You can talk all day, but my mind is made up."
2. Aggressor	Struggles for status by deflating the status of others; boasts; criticizes.	"Wow, that's really swell! You turkeys have botched things again." "Your constant bickering is responsible for this mess. Let me tell you how you ought to do it."
3. Deserter	Withdraws in some way; remains indifferent, aloof, sometimes formal; daydreams; wanders from the subject; engages in irrelevant side conversations.	"Oh, I suppose that's all right . . . I really don't care."
4. Dominator	Interrupts and embarks on long monologues; is authoritative; tries to monopolize the group's time.	"Mike, you're just off base. What we should do is this. First . . ."
5. Recognition seeker	Attempts to gain attention in an exaggerated manner; usually boasts about past accomplishments; relates irrelevant personal experiences, usually in an attempt to gain sympathy.	"That reminds me of a guy I used to know . . ." "Let me tell you how I handled old Marris . . ."
6. Playboy	Displays a lack of involvement in the group through inappropriate humor, horseplay, or cynicism.	"Why try to convince these guys? Let's just get the mob to snuff them out." "Hey, Carla, wanna be my roommate at the sales conference?"

To support a general climate of consistency and stability, an organization and its parts also need a mission. A mission statement clarifies the organization's direction and priorities by defining

- the business that you're in
- what the boundaries of your business are
- who your customers are both outside and inside the organization
- how the various departments will work together

- the key results to be accomplished
- how achievement of these key results will be measured

As the leader of his or her organization, it is the manager's responsibility to initiate the creation or refinement of the team's vision and mission. Often senior managers will schedule an off-site for the purpose of outlining these fundamental strategies. To set the stage for effectively fostering the development of a common vision among direct reports, the manager prepares and presents an analysis of internal and external factors affecting the business. This does not have to be highly detailed since the managers should participate in the process. However, it should include such items as the following:

- Who is the competition?
- What are our resources?
- What is our market?
- What are other issues with vendors and suppliers?
- What are our customer concerns?
- What are our legal or other regulatory concerns?
- Do we have global issues?
- What is the general financial outlook?
- How deep is the talent pool in the organization?
- Are there organizational culture issues?
- What are the relevant elements of your management style?

An example agenda for such a meeting is presented as Appendix A at the end of this book.

Another very effective exercise is force field analysis, which is a general-purpose diagnostic and problem-solving technique. It is based on the principle that in any situation there are forces that drive or push for change as well as forces that restrain or hinder change. If the forces offset one another completely, the result is equilibrium and status quo. In a situation where changes need to be made based on a reorganization, or if the executive has been recently appointed to the new position and has the charge of making some changes, the application of force field analysis will help to develop a strategic plan as well as assert control over the group process. Force field analysis is discussed in detail with examples in Chapter 11.

In addition to articulating a mission and setting a vision, managers need to communicate direction and priorities to their people. When staff members are clear about the organizational priorities, it enables them to make appropriate decisions about which issues to tackle and in which order.

Once the vision has been articulated and the mission statement completed, meetings are set with direct reports to explore individual goals and objectives. Managers should clearly indicate their priorities and be prepared to negotiate and make adjustments based on input from the staff. Holding periodic update meetings to review the group's progress against the goals that were set is a good follow-up. One way of managing those meetings effectively and providing your direct reports with a feeling of empowerment is to shift the agenda responsibility from one member to another for each of the meetings going forward. In this way each subgroup has the feeling that they are being provided with an opportunity to get their issues on the agenda.

Clarify Roles and Responsibilities

Another major factor with consistency is being clear about the roles and responsibilities of the group as a whole as well as the individuals in that group. Clear delineation of responsibilities builds ownership. Also, because of the nature of change, it will be necessary to continually revisit and, in some cases, reshuffle roles and responsibilities. This clarification is an ongoing process in a dynamic organization. Open and frank discussion about differences in role expectations among your direct reports should be encouraged. In order to be perceived as a strong leader in those instances where consensus is not possible or appropriate, the manager needs to make a decision and let the team know the rationale for that decision.

Market the Mission

A consistent leader dedicates effort toward presenting the group or department's mission to the larger organization. Not only should managers be primary spokespeople for the efforts and achievements for organizations; they should also select employees from within the ranks to represent the group's point of view through presentations to other groups in the organization.

Focus on Personal and Professional Development

Consistency is also demonstrated through a manager's focus on the personal and professional development of the people, including training and providing access to both internal and external resources to raise competency levels and job satisfaction. This also serves to carry the message and priorities to the full extent of the manager's organization. It enables the setting of consistent standards and allows the people in the organization to feel comfortable about being on the right track. When the opportunities arise to provide individual coaching, the manager's interactions with the staff members should have a future focus rather than being merely evaluative. When criticism is warranted, it should be consistent with the standards that have been clearly communicated to the individual in question.

ORGANIZATIONAL LEADERS ARE COMMITTED

The nature of modern organizations requires a leadership approach that depends more on influence than on giving orders. A major factor in the amount of influence a manager exerts within his or her organization and beyond is the recognition of the manager's commitment to particular issues and points of view. Successful leaders command attention. They demonstrate an eagerness to present their points of view. They are firm and direct when stating expectations or confronting issues or ideas that run contrary to their established thinking. Some managers confuse assertiveness with aggressiveness. The simple difference is that while both behaviors have confrontational elements, assertiveness focuses on the issue, whereas aggressiveness attacks the individual.

Commitment is also demonstrated by the rapidity of the response to issues. Effective managers address concerns as soon as possible. Delaying response, even for the best of reasons, can often be interpreted as a lack of commitment.

Communicating Commitment

Commitment is shown through clarifying and communicating the vision. The more clear and compelling the vision, the easier it is for others to understand and endorse it. Commitment is also demonstrated through enthusiasm. The more excited and energetic managers are about meeting their goals, the more committed others are likely to be in supporting them. Enthusiasm is displayed by conveying how important the goals are and how pleased you are that people are willing to pitch in and work with you.

Group situations are an excellent opportunity for managers to demonstrate their commitment and to have impact on a large number of people. They state their opinions forcefully and don't hesitate to voice their thoughts or label them as their own. A good strategy for a manager is to look for opportunities to lead groups outside of the immediate organization.

Commitment is also demonstrated through interactions with the management above. When a manager recognizes that a decision from upper management might have a negative impact on his or her area, it is dealt with directly and clearly by presenting upper management with the impact the decision will have by citing tangible consequences. If it is necessary to make concessions, they should be positioned as being important to the larger organization. People's trust in their manager is enhanced when the manager's motives appear directed at benefiting the entire organization.

Commitment to Teamwork

Commitment is shown not only through adherence to issues and positions in the organization but also through a demonstration of the manager's commitment to the group and teamwork in general. As the leader, a manager's actions and policies affect the overall ability of the group to work together. The most effective managers

- create structures that are conducive to both work groups and teams
- encourage and reward cooperation rather than competition between different work units
- provide the means for groups to communicate their goals and objectives to one another and ensure that they are mutually supportive
- provide subgroups with the authority to act upon their decisions
- set an example by demonstrating group leadership as well as being an effective group member
- acknowledge and celebrate work group and team accomplishments

These actions not only demonstrate a commitment to this process but keep the motivation and momentum going.

ORGANIZATIONAL LEADERS ARE COURAGEOUS

Today's environment demands that leaders make decisions that involve risk and take a stand in the face of ambiguity or conflict. Successful leaders confront problems directly and take action based on what they believe is right. As a result, they win the respect and commitment of others by standing up for what they believe and making the tough decisions. They also stand behind their people who take risks and make difficult decisions. Taking risks in any situation requires conviction if a particular action is going against the mainstream or is not widely accepted. And yet it is often the willingness of an individual to take risks that stands out most when he or she is being evaluated as a leader.

What Is Important to You?

Ask yourself what is really important to you, what is worth fighting for, standing up for. Think about the legacy you want to leave your organization, what things or qualities you want to be remembered for. Identifying what is most important to you establishes the foundation for leading courageously when it matters. Look for situations in which others may be overly concerned about taking a stand but where you strongly believe in the correctness of your position based on your convictions and your understanding of the situation. This is an opportunity to develop a rationale and make your position clear to others. Rather than waiting for these opportunities to come to you, you need to actively look for opportunities to stand up for what you believe.

Take Action

Managers are often faced with situations in which taking the most appropriate course of action carries with it a backlash of complaints, problems, and negative reactions. Successful leaders will not avoid taking action in these situations; they confront the tough issues head-on, since they understand in the long run no one benefits by ignoring issues that must be addressed and resolved. In fact, more respect and concern are shown for people when tough issues are confronted rather than ignored. Obviously, managers want to choose their battles carefully, since they can't possibly do everything. But it is especially critical for them to address the issues that get in the way of their mission.

It is often a good idea to enlist the input from direct reports regarding the areas most important for taking risks. When important individual or team issues are brought to attention, it is critical for a manager to respond quickly. Indecisiveness may result in the perception that the manager cannot make the tough choices or take a stand on issues. Some managers are concerned that taking a stand on a particular issue will cause others to dislike them. Even the most popular leaders are not liked by everyone, but even if a person is not liked, his or her ideas may be valued. Consistently seeking approval projects to others that a manager lacks confidence. Risk taking is discussed openly with direct reports. Model the behavior for them. Talk through the problems and describe how you arrived at the decision you chose.

Embrace Change

Perhaps one of the most courageous actions a leader can take is to embrace change. The willingness and ability to champion change will go a long way toward determining anyone's effectiveness as a manager in today's competitive business environment. Successful change efforts require the commitment and support of key individuals throughout the organization to plan, manage, and implement the change. Managers need to develop a strategy to get the necessary people on board. In some cases, this will require courage, since there are risks involved in suggesting change actions.

Meetings need to be held with each person individually to explain the rationale for the change, the potential benefits, and the implementation plans. To maximize buy-in and minimize resistance, managers need to involve others in this process. When employees feel that they are valued participants in planning and implementing the change, they are more likely to be motivated toward successful completion. Solicit and use the input from the team, peers, and upper management when planning any change effort. If the change means significant loss for some individuals or areas of the organization, don't downplay the message and pretend that it is anything other than what it is. Just deliver the message including the support that will be provided during the transition period. Be straightforward and honest about the implications of the change.

Beyond just perceiving the need for a change in ongoing processes and procedures, successful leaders reach beyond their everyday assignments and responsibilities and identify new initiatives and improvements within the organization. They create clear and compelling visions of the changes that are necessary. They identify the people who can help make the change a reality, and they take the initiative for sharing their ideas, conclusions, and reasons for excitement and commitment with others.

THE ROLE OF STYLE IN LEADERSHIP

Style can be characterized in two different ways. First, it can be observed as a communication style of an individual who aspires to leadership. On this basis, style relates to verbal and nonverbal behaviors that contribute to the leader's total effect. The second way to look at leadership style describes style as an approach to leadership. This style dimension is determined by the pattern of behaviors that a particular individual uses when applying leadership.

Research into the effect of style on the emergence of leadership has pointed out that group members whose communication was perceived as quiet, tentative, or vague were viewed as uncommitted to the group and not knowledgeable about the group's task. Those who exhibited these behaviors were quickly eliminated as potential leaders because it was felt that they did not contribute ideas or help organize the group. Those who did emerge as leaders made more attempts to suggest procedures for the group and thus help get the group organized. In addition, their participation profiles were high in maintenance roles like contributing to procedural issues and also fairly high in task roles like information giving and seeking but were low in stating opinions.[3]

There has been a tendency to think of biological gender as being a determinant of group leadership. Males were perceived to more likely emerge as leaders than females. However, more recently, gender has been a much less important factor, and recent studies find no significant differences in the amount of communication style behaviors contributed by men or women. In these studies it appears that the type of task did not influence the emergence of leadership but that group members' individual abilities to contribute to the task and their commitment to the group goal regardless of sex were associated with their emergence as leaders.

Despite the fact that leadership is contextual, that is, a person may be perceived as a leader in one situation and not in another, it seems equally clear that people with the ability to adapt their behaviors and who possess communication skills that help clarify the group's task and motivate other members will exert influence on groups. Through careful self-monitoring, anyone who aspires to leadership will identify the needs of the particular group and be flexible enough to adapt to those needs.

Style Approaches

The classical description of leadership approaches includes three basic styles:

1. *democratic leadership*, which encourages members to participate in group decisions including policy-making decisions
2. *laissez-faire leadership*, which takes almost no initiative for structuring a group but is responsive to inquiries from members,
3. *autocratic leadership*, which exerts tight control over the group including making assignments, directing all verbal interaction, and giving orders

Autocratic and democratic styles of leadership correspond closely with the *Theory X* and *Theory Y* assumptions about humans described by management theorist Douglas McGregor.[4] Theory X assumes that people don't like to work and must therefore be compelled by a strong, controlling leader who supervises their work closely. Theory Y makes a different assumption: People work as naturally as they play and are creative problem solvers who like to take charge of their own work. Leaders who accept the assumption of Theory Y behave democratically by providing only as much structure as the group needs and allowing members to participate fully in decision making and other aspects of the group's work. Research on these two approaches has been relatively consistent. The democratically led groups are generally more satisfied than the autocratically led groups, and most people in Western culture prefer democratic groups. Other findings show that autocratic groups tend to work harder in the presence of the leader, but they also experience more incidents of aggressiveness and apathy. Comparison between democratic groups and laissez-faire groups shows that groups perform better with some structure and coordination, particularly with regard to problem solving. Although leadership that provides some structure appears to be the most desirable for both productivity and satisfaction, there are contingent factors such as cultural values that affect how much structure and control a particular group seems to need.

Contingency Theories of Leadership

These contingent factors have given rise to contingency theories or approaches relating to leadership. These approaches acknowledge that there are several factors including members, skills, experience, cultural values, the actual tasks of the group, and the time available to achieve those tasks that affect the type of leadership likely to be effective. The selection of how a leader may structure a particular meeting is dependent upon the same contingent factors that we take into account for the larger group as well. It is not necessary to provide an exhaustive discussion of the various contingency approaches in order to identify those issues that are most germane for a manager to develop leadership style. However, a brief summary is useful as a jumping-off place for listing these attributes.

The Functions Approach. Functional approaches attempt to define specific behaviors to be performed by leaders. Without naming leadership, the work of Benne and Sheats discussed earlier in this chapter falls into this category. B. Aubrey Fischer sorts through the task and maintenance roles and identifies four functions performed by leaders:

1. providing sufficient information and having the ability to process and handle a large amount of information
2. enacting a variety of functions needed within the group (e.g., task and maintenance roles)
3. helping group members make sense of decisions and actions performed within the organization by supplying acceptable rationale
4. focusing on the here and now and stopping the group from jumping to unwarranted conclusions or adopting stock answers too quickly[5]

Fiedler's Contingency Model. Theorist Fred Fiedler takes a somewhat different view. Rather than seeing leadership as a relatively open and adaptable behavior, he views leaders as people who are relatively inflexible. The leadership behaviors are preferred by the individual and are used more effectively than other selective behaviors might be. Fiedler's contingency model concludes that there are three factors upon which appropriate leader behaviors are contingent:

1. the relationship between the leader and the people being led
2. the structure of the task or the responsibilities of the group
3. the leader's position in terms of legitimate power over the group[6]

In Fiedler's view there are certain individual characteristics that make people suited for leadership only in certain types of contingencies, so it is more productive to match prospective leaders to situations than to try to change the individual style. However, this suggests that the tasks and responsibilities of the group will remain relatively stable. This may have been more the case in 1967, when Fiedler's book was written. In today's environment of rampant reorganization, it is not uncommon for an individual who is designated as a leader because of his or her executive position in the organization to find himself or herself responsible for a wide variety of suborganizations within a relatively short period of time.

Hersey and Blanchard's Situational Model. The widely accepted situational leadership model developed by Hersey and Blanchard moves in the opposite direction. They believe that people are flexible enough to adapt their behavior to meet the needs of many groups. The most effective leaders, in their view, are able to assess both the relationship issues and task orientation associated with applying leadership strategies. Not only does the leader need to adjust to the overall needs of the group; he or she also has to have the ability to adapt to the needs of the members of the group at all points during the life of the group. It assumes a deep knowledge and understanding of each individual's needs and competencies. Hersey and Blanchard provide a very useful construct for small group leadership. However, it becomes unwieldy for leaders of large organizations to attempt to understand everyone in the organization at that level.

The Communication Competency Approach. The communication competency model grew out of the felt need to account for contingencies without overwhelming the leader with complexity. The approach is the result of work done on small group leadership, but many of the principles that derive from the competency approach are applicable to leaders of large organizations as well. The communication competency model is based on the assumptions that leadership involves behaviors that help a group overcome obstacles to achieving their goals and that leadership occurs through the process of communication. It is a contingency approach because it assumes that the actual context facing the leader and the group is constantly shifting so that different competencies may be needed at different points.

The limitation of any competency approach lies in the fact that in order to be a true competency the behavior must be both observable and measurable by some criteria. Many of the qualities that we associate with leadership are not so easily discernible.[7] Taking this into account, the competency model provides us with a springboard for seven additional factors that we can associate with effective leadership.

1. Effective leaders are active communicators who can express their ideas clearly and concisely; they speak clearly and fluently; they have a facility in verbalizing problems, goals, values, ideas, and solutions.

2. Effective leaders communicate the group's vision and mission. Perhaps, more than anything else, the way they communicate reveals an extensive knowledge about the issues and an understanding of the procedures that facilitate accomplishment.

3. Effective leaders are skilled in coordinating the information and ideas of others. They have good analytic skills and apply critical thinking that leads to a thorough evaluation and integration of the information they receive. They provide structure to unorganized information, ask probing questions to bring out pertinent information, and help others focus on activities relevant to the overall goal.

4. Effective leaders own their opinions but express them provisionally. They suspend judgment and encourage full consideration of minority viewpoints. They tend to withhold their own opinions about the actions to be taken until they have heard the offerings of others. By reserving judgment these leaders are perceived as being open-minded.

5. Effective leaders appear to be group centered. Successful leaders articulate the vision and the mission in such a way as to inspire a desire for an eventual commitment to the accomplishment of the goals and objectives. Furthermore, their personal commitment is clear to all, and they are willing to confront individuals who appear more self-centered than group-centered.

6. Effective leaders demonstrate respect for others. They are sensitive to non-verbal signals and the feelings these signify. They perceive the needs and goals of individual members and adjust behaviors to these needs. They also display common courtesy.

7. Effective leaders share in the success of the organization. Although leadership carries with it the temptation to take credit for the accomplishments of the group, effective leaders share as equals both within the group and when dealing with outsiders. They credit people for their accomplishments and work with individuals to develop their leadership competencies. They are good at expressing appreciation.

LEADING FROM A DISTANCE

Managing virtual work groups, or even traditional groups that have interactions with virtual participants, have both similar and unique requirements to management challenges in a traditional setting. The basic qualities of leadership already described here are applicable to groups that may be fully or partially dispersed and have little or no opportunity to meet face-to-face.

Difficulty of scheduling, timing, work interaction, and general communication can be significantly magnified in the virtual or remote situation. A leader's ability to be effective under these conditions requires confident and deliberate actions to keep people on track. A key to effectively leading in this manner is to get to know the members of the group as much as possible. What are their needs and concerns? Their level of technical expertise? The level of supervision they need to feel comfortable? Also, an effective leader will select the combinations of technology best suited to the needs of both the project and the participants.

Another key is to limit the expectations and objectives for each virtual session to segments of a problem or issue that can be dealt with in the time available. For all its supposed efficiency, electronic interaction takes much more time to accomplish the same ends than a face-to-face meeting. Despite the drawbacks, virtual groups are an essential part of today's working world. Leading in this environment emphasizes the need for building trust, creating a feeling of community, setting clear objectives, praising individual success, coaching as needed, and finding opportunities for the group to interact in ways that will enable them to see one another as human beings.

Leadership in today's complex and ever-changing organizations is not for everyone. The old adage that "it's lonely at the top" has never been more true than it is today. In my role as an executive coach, I often find that the executive's greatest need at times is to just have someone to talk to and share with. Much is expected of today's leaders:

- They have to be individual contributors in a significant way.
- They have to be effective communicators.
- They have to balance toughness and compassion.
- They have to be accessible without being overwhelmed.
- They have to be energetic and driving without bringing too much stress to others.
- They need to appear courageous, committed, and consistent to those that report to them and to those to whom they report as well.

NOTES

1. Ernest G. Bormann, *Small Group Discussion: Theory and Practice*, 3rd ed. (New York: Harper & Row, 1990), 205–214, 291–292; John C. Geier, "A Trait Approach to the Study of Leadership in Small Groups," *Journal of Communication* 17 (1967): 316–323.

2. Kenneth D. Benne and Paul Sheats, "Functional Roles of Group Members," *Journal of Social Issues* 4 (Spring 1948): 41–49.

3. Deborah C. Baker, "A Qualitative and Quantitative Analysis of Verbal Style and the Elimination of Potential Leaders in Small Groups," *Communication Quarterly* 39 (Winter 1990): 13–26.

4. Douglas McGregor, *The Human Side of Enterprise*, rev. ed. (New York: McGraw-Hill/Irwin, 1985).

5. B. Aubrey Fisher, "Leadership as Medium: Treating Complexity in Group Communication Research," *Small Group Behavior* 16 (1985): 167–196.

6. Fred E. Fiedler, *A Theory of Leadership Effectiveness* (New York: McGraw-Hill, 1967).

7. J. Kevin Barge and Randy Y. Hirokawa, "Toward a Communication Competency of Group Leadership," *Small Group Behavior* 20 (1989): 167–189.

CHAPTER 4

Types of Meetings

A manager's approach to a meeting will be affected by why the meeting is taking place. We often err in trying to accomplish too much or focus on some issues too early.

KEY CONCEPTS

- Meetings have a prevailing purpose.
- Managers are judged as facilitators.
- Meeting types need to be differentiated.
- Determine when to get involved.

In the preceding chapters, we have discussed issues that affect managing group process in broad terms. Looking at the organization as a system and the various roles that groups play in today's organizations, we find that leadership strategies are an important foundation for managing group process. Particularly when examining systems theory and leadership components, we can see how various approaches and strategies can affect the climate and performance of the total group or full organization.

With this chapter we begin to take a narrower view of group process. We have already established that today's executives spend half or more of their productive time in meetings, often as facilitators. The overall impression that a manager makes on the organization as a whole can frequently be determined by how that manager is perceived as a meeting facilitator. Managing meetings puts the manager in the spotlight. It provides opportunities for a variety of people in the organization to observe and make judgments about a wide range of competencies.

Here are some of the judgment factors that people will use to assess a manager's performance as a facilitator. Did the facilitator

- define the objective for the meeting?
- select the appropriate participants?
- make effective contact with participants before the meeting?
- schedule appropriate meeting space and equipment?
- prepare an effective agenda?
- start on time?
- follow the agenda as presented?
- manage everyone's use of time effectively?
- control the direction of the discussion?
- create a working climate?
- elicit participation from all members?
- actively work to resolve conflicts and to coordinate ideas?
- summarize and clarify actions to be taken?
- take any actions that are his or her responsibility?
- follow up on the action items of others?

Facilitating meetings appears to be an integral part of any executive's landscape. However, the skills of facilitation are not just a subset of management skills. Often the same executives who are charged with presenting the big picture or being a leader will find that they need to do things in the facilitator role that appear to be in direct conflict with what they might normally do in a traditional executive role. The most successful executives today have the flexibility to move between three distinguishing roles. They need to be leaders, take the long-term view, set the tone, and point their people in the right direction. They need to pay attention to the here and now, plan effectively, and set the pace. They need to be facilitators and help the work get done.

Getting work done is what facilitators help others to do. They provide methods that support both accomplishing tasks and helping individuals work together more effectively. Depending on the situation, one aspect may be emphasized more than the other. Good facilitation helps people make the connection between the quality of their work and the way they treat each other as they do the work.

Any one meeting can have characteristics that are associated with a variety of dynamics. Portions of the meeting may be devoted to providing information; other segments might be spent problem solving, while the meeting may end with a decision. However, most meetings have a prevailing purpose. In this chapter we will distinguish between various types of meetings and illustrate how a skilled facilitator might respond based on the prevailing purpose of the meeting. The prevailing purpose for meetings falls into one of the following categories.

- information-giving meeting
- fact-finding meeting
- persuasion meeting
- problem-solving and/or decision-making meeting
- focus group meeting

INFORMATION-GIVING MEETING

The president of the company calls a meeting of his direct reports. He begins the meeting by announcing that current trends in the market have created a need for a change in direction. Profitability is beginning to suffer, and future projections based on the current direction are not promising. He asks the chief financial officer to provide some specific details on the current outlook. Using a prepared handout incorporating tables, charts, and graphs, she walks the executives through the financial picture. She highlights the buildup in inventories and what appears to be a drop in demand for one of the company's core products. At that point in the presentation she asks the manufacturing vice president, the source of her information, to elaborate on that particular point. The manufacturing vice president underscores the need for better inventory control and highlights changes in the order flow. The company president asks the sales and marketing vice president to talk a little bit about the downturn in sales. She confirms that several major customers have slowed orders for the product in question. Each vice president is then charged with the task of outlining some steps they feel can be taken in each of their areas to offset the current loss in business. A time for a new meeting is scheduled for the following week, and the meeting is adjourned.

Could possible solutions have been raised and debated at this meeting? Probably so. Would that have been the best use of everyone's time? Probably not. Much of the information, and in particular the situation of the company as a whole, probably did not come as a surprise to the participants. Many important details and an understanding of various perspectives can be developed at this information-giving meeting. The situation above describes a circumstance where the information being provided is not particularly good news. Without developing an alternative scenario, you can probably see how the circumstances could be quite the opposite. For example, the president could have gathered his direct reports to tell them how the company had exceeded projections for the quarter and that this was due primarily to an increasing demand for one of their key products. While the tone and some of the dynamics of the meeting might have been different, the structure and process—and the intent—would have been the same.

When preparing for an information meeting, a manager needs to be sensitive to what information the group is ready to use. Whether the news is going to be good or bad, it doesn't help to avalanche the group with too much information. If this meeting will be followed up with other meetings for problem-solving and decision-making purposes, select only two or three observations that will stimulate the thinking and future discussions that will be held. If members of the group feel a need for more information, let them ask for it during the meeting.

During the meeting be particularly careful about singling out individuals for praise or blame. If one individual deserves particular acknowledgment because he or she has made an exceptional contribution, schedule a special event, even if it is only a brief gathering at the end of the day or a luncheon where it is clear to everyone, including the individual involved, that praise and celebration are the only issues on the table.

FACT-FINDING MEETING

Continuing with our current scenario, we might assume that each vice president needing to outline some steps to improve the situation scheduled some meetings with their direct reports. One can envision that the vice president of sales would have asked her sales managers to collect data and anecdotal information from their various territories to gain some insight into the current downturn in business. She might also ask the sales managers to provide realistic projections for business going forward in the near term.

In his fact-finding meetings, the manufacturing vice president uncovers some processes and procedures that provide for automatic ordering of certain materials based on time intervals rather than stock on hand. It also appears that some orders for material have been instigated by members of the sales team who anticipated closing pieces of business that did not happen. In the meantime, they felt that when the orders came through they needed to have materials on hand. At the same time, the financial officer is trying to look beyond the current problems and establish an approach to inventory control that works best from both a supply and financial standpoint. She charges her direct reports with the responsibility of determining best practices in their industry for inventory control.

It is safe to say that although the primary purpose of these meetings is fact finding, suggestions are placed on the table, and solutions or potential solutions are argued vigorously among the parties. However, that is not the purpose of these meetings, and as the facilitator, each vice president must manage the communication flow and dynamics to keep everyone focused as much as possible on the intelligence-gathering purpose of the meeting.

PERSUASION MEETING

Persuasion meetings can occur in many forms. Perhaps what comes most quickly to mind are those meetings held with clients and prospects of the organization to present a proposal and hopefully convince the members of the meeting to adopt it. However, persuasion meetings of all kinds also take place that are made up entirely of the organization's employees. For example, a particular department may need persuading to either take on or relinquish certain responsibilities. Multiple factors around change management issues also fall into this category: adapting to new systems, procedures, and working relationships.

Following along with our current scenario, one of the sales and marketing vice president's direct reports has turned up some disturbing data indicating that there are too few prospects in the funnel to offset the loss of current customers and the lower volumes being experienced. By selectively interviewing several of his salespeople, he determines that too much time is being spent with current clients or unproductive prospects and not enough time is being allotted for new business development. He calls a meeting of his sales staff and solicits their input about what can be done to generate new leads as well as what kind of support they might require in order to enhance the possibility of closing new business. As an added incentive he hires an outside consultant to speak to the group about prospecting norms and the expectations for converting new leads into solid business. The sales group is also put through an exercise so that each salesperson can determine how he or she stands with regard to generally expected prospecting behaviors. The session ends with some action planning resulting in projections and commitments by each salesperson for new business development going forward.

PROBLEM-SOLVING AND/OR DECISION-MAKING MEETING

Much has been written about so-called rational actor problem-solving and decision-making models. While these have been discredited to some extent in terms of their real-life application in organizational decision making, the rational actor model continues to provide a good blueprint for structuring and managing problem-solving and decision-making activity.[1] The argument against rational actor models is that they make a few assumptions that are not practical in today's workplace. First, they assume that it is possible to collect all or almost all the pertinent information needed in order to make a particular decision. Second, they require that all of the people involved in the decision process agree on the criteria to be used and the weight to be provided to each criterion. Third, decision making using this model is relegated to an exercise of the intellect—the assumption being that the correct decision will be so obvious that it will carry with it inherent agreement from all parties involved.

Critics of rational actor models point out that rarely, if ever, in today's fast-paced environment do individuals or groups have the opportunity or the means to collect all of the potentially useful information involved in a decision. This point of view asserts that decisions are made by using some combination of information, experience, and risk tolerance. The process might go along the lines of: "This problem looks very much like one I have experienced before with some exceptions. Therefore, based on my experience with the previous problem and the success of the outcome, I will take the risk that the same solution will apply here." Current management practices often appear to consist of managers equipped with solutions ranging through the organizations looking for the problems that fit their expertise and experience.

The danger of this approach is that there is a tendency for the competency of the "problem solver" to define the problem. Or, as the old adage goes, when you put a hammer in the hand of a child, everything begins to look like a nail. This provides another compelling reason for top managers to become more involved in managing group process. Because of what is currently happening in the business environment, midlevel managers are being assigned responsibilities that lie outside their experience and proven ability. Solutions they bring with them from their prior orientation have great potential to misfire in the new set of circumstances.

Let's rejoin our ongoing scenario. With fact finding completed and reasonable time for internal discussion, the president schedules a problem-solving meeting. He ensures that ample time will be provided to consider alternatives by scheduling a full day off-site to minimize interruptions and command everyone's attention. Each vice president is provided with the opportunity to make a 20-minute presentation covering his or her analysis of the problem and proposed solutions.

Following the presentations, the president places along the front wall of the room headings that represent the components of the problem at hand: Inventories, Decreased Demand, Productivity, Receivables, Product Mix. The vice presidents are then challenged to arrange their solutions under each of the headings, creating a composite of all of the suggested actions and where they will have impact. The exercise also highlights areas where there are no solutions or where there are conflicting solutions. The group then works the rest of the day to fill in, refine, and consolidate their approach to the overall problem. In this case, the president has employed a tool called an "affinity diagram" to help facilitate understanding, discussion, and full participation by all group members. He has taken an active role in the process, demonstrated his control of the process, and hopefully, arrived at a consensus that everyone can live with.

FOCUS GROUP MEETING

A primary tool for marketing and advertising research, the focus group has also become an effective way to gather information about problems, interests, and concerns of employees, customers, and the general public. The range of focus group approaches is broad. A focus group can be unstructured and informal, or it can be highly structured, depending on the kind of information being sought. As an information-gathering tool, it is most effective for collecting qualitative data, such as likes and dislikes, values, attitudes, beliefs, and felt needs. In a business setting, focus groups can help determine customer interest in a product or concerns about the company. Focus groups with employees can uncover needs for training and development, changes in compensation and benefits, and underlying issues relating to the general morale and quality of work life in an organization.

The vice president of marketing in our scenario might do well to conduct some focus groups with current and potential customers to determine the best approach to product development, presentation, and product mix. The president might want to conduct some focus groups with midlevel managers and supervisors to determine how some of the proposed changes will impact on morale and productivity.

When conducting a focus group, it is a good idea to build in some controls or cross-checks to confirm or disconfirm the qualitative data being collected. The dynamics of groups being what they are, sometimes one or two dominant members can skew the data toward their point of view by causing dissenters to either conform or withhold their true opinions. Having focus group members fill out a questionnaire or using some other individual response instruments will provide the facilitator with material that either supports or denies the focus group results. One method I have used effectively is a card sort. With this approach, 10 to 15 cards are prepared, each containing a value statement relating to the issue at hand. Following is a set of value statements I used to evaluate issues in a financial services marketing department.

1. I am looking forward to changes in the company.
2. I view the launching of new products as an opportunity.
3. I feel comfortable in a marketing environment.
4. Lines of communication are open between myself and management.

5. I would describe myself as a marketing professional.

6. I am planning to leave the company soon.

7. Communication between departments is very good.

8. Upper management is providing clear direction and leadership.

9. I am uncertain about my future.

10. I am happy with things as they are.

11. I need more responsibility and authority.

12. Management is not concerned about my problems.

13. I would rather have a different job than the one I have now.

14. I view the launching of new products as an added burden.

15. Many of my colleagues are incompetent or unprofessional.

Each participant in the group was given a pack of cards with these statements printed one to a card. At the end of the session, they were asked to arrange the cards in the order they felt best reflected their true feelings. The statements that they agreed most strongly with were placed at the top, while those they disagreed with were placed toward the bottom. A rubber band was used to secure each pack, and they were randomly collected to maintain anonymity.

This particular analysis supported some conclusions derived from the focus group session and called others into question. The group discussion was very "politically correct," since the participants had some uncertainty about their own future. However, the card sort indicated that the group was not satisfied with the level of communication with management or between departments, and they were not happy with the direction and leadership they were receiving from upper management.

Participating in focus groups with customers and employees is another way that today's executive can get a real feel for what is happening in and out of the organization. In fact, participation in all these types of meetings will serve to minimize isolation and provide quality, firsthand understanding of what needs to be done for the organization to become or remain successful.

The types of meetings discussed in this chapter may not represent every purposeful gathering that takes place in an organization. Some meetings may be purely transactional in nature, allowing people to air grievances and mend relationships. Others may be meetings among peers negotiating priorities and resources. On occasion, it may be important for managers to be involved in these as well. However, when making a judgment about becoming directly involved as a facilitator, a manager should select those group sessions that have a strategic focus.

NOTE

1. Charles Conrad, *Strategic Organizational Communication: Toward the Twenty-First Century*, 3rd ed. (Fort Worth, TX: Harcourt Brace College Publishers, 1994), 302–305.

PART II

Getting Things Done in Groups

THE SIX CORE SKILLS FOR FACILITATING

There are a number of ways to classify communication events. We could look at the motivation driving the event, the participants, even the environment. However, despite the many simultaneous factors in play (nonverbals, ambient noise), facilitation remains primarily a linear activity with a beginning, a middle, and an end. The skill sets presented here are focused on facilitation behaviors but could be applied universally for any type of interpersonal interaction.

There are six core skills related to gaining and maintaining control over the group environment (Figure II.1). Regardless of the type of meeting a manager is facilitating, he or she will be using these core skills both to move the group forward and to control the dynamics of the interaction:

1. initiating an interaction, opening a meeting, presenting a new idea, laying the groundwork for moving forward, beginning to build new relationships

2. questioning to develop information relevant to the group's needs and to involve the participants in the group process

3. active listening to demonstrate understanding of the issues or needs of the group

4. responding with proposals and recommendations that are based on the identified needs of the group and the project

5. resolving differences or problems; clarifying any misunderstandings

Figure II.1
Interpersonal Competency Matrix

	CONSULTING (Influencing)	INTERVIEW (Fact-finding)	SELLING (Persuasion)	NEGOTIATION (Bargaining)	COACHING (Mentoring)	FACILITATING (Leadership)	PRESENTING
INITIATE	• Affiliation • Role clarification	• Rapport • Orientation • Control	• Prospecting • Rapport • Orientation • Control	• Identify situation • Establish opening positions	• Approach • Rapport • Orientation	• Rapport • Orientation • Empowerment	• Attention • Goodwill • Orientation
QUESTION	• Problem definition • Data gathering • Risk issues	• Test assumptions • Probe • Confirm	• Identify needs • Raise concerns	• Explore needs and concerns	• Explore needs and concerns • Ask for solutions	• Explore issues • Objectives • Stimulate interaction	• Key points • Organizational strategy • Hypothetical questions
ACTIVELY LISTEN	• Monitor feedback • Evaluate concerns • Clarify and confirm	• Build relationship • Encourage full response	• Build relationship • Clarify and confirm	• Clarify and confirm	• Build relationship • Clarify and confirm	• Coordinate • Support • Orient • Clarify	• Monitor feedback • Evaluate
RESPOND	• Motivate • Present issues • Recommendations	• Mirror • Provide information • Present feedback	• Connect needs with features • Present solutions as benefits	• Propose/explore options	• Evaluate solutions • Suggest additional solutions	• Evaluation • Process/tools	• Adapt • Focus on needs and benefits • Motivate
RESOLVE	• Clarify • Manage expectations	• Manage objections	• Manage objections	• Problem solving • Bargaining • Trade off	• Problem solving	• Gatekeeping • Harmonizing • Consensus	• Clarification • Expansion • Application • Example
COMMIT	• Summarize • Agreement • Implementation	• Summarize • Next steps	• Summarize • Close	• Acceptance • Agreement	• Agreement • Action plan	• Summarize • Action plan	• Summarize • Action plan

6. committing/closing by getting agreement on action plans and establishing next steps

The following chapters in this section will discuss each of these core competencies in relation to effectively managing group process.

CHAPTER 5

Initiating Group Process

All interpersonal communication processes have beginnings. Often these beginnings are seen as just a means to "get to the important stuff." In fact, beginning well is extremely important, and the skills associated with it require study and practice. Beginning effectively puts the facilitator in control of the communication process and moves events in the direction he or she wants them to go. Beginnings occur at the outset of a facilitation event and also during the event when transitioning to a new issue. The skills needed relate to meeting, greeting, and gaining and maintaining control of the meeting process.

KEY CONCEPTS

- Introducing yourself and group members.
- Demonstrating interest.
- Establishing rapport.
- Creating trust.
- Building a level of comfort.
- Beginning to develop a professional relationship.
- Orienting the group to various stages of the meeting process.
- Maintaining control of the interpersonal interaction.

Some situations may arise spontaneously that call for managers to apply effective facilitation skills, but this is not normally the case.

When a manager finds himself or herself engaged in facilitation, it is because he or she has an agenda—wants to achieve some specific objectives—and has some ideas about how the meeting should go. In effect, even the most enlightened managers are susceptible to the power syndrome. Their hearts may be saying, "I want to work with these people to arrive at the best decisions and empower them to take the initiative to make important things happen." But somewhere in their minds there is a voice that urges, "I am the manager, after all, and if this doesn't work, I'm the person on the line. I think I know what needs to be done here, and I need to move these people toward my point of view." When this voice is loud and clear, there is little need for facilitation. Simply make the decision and issue a directive or conduct an information-giving meeting and inform everyone of the decision. A manager who uses meetings as a way to give orders rapidly loses trust and respect. Direct reports begin to feel that they are wasting valuable time, since their input is not truly sought after or heeded.

There are many times, however, when input from others is important to shape a decision or test a hypothesis even when the manager feels strongly about a particular action. So a balance needs to be struck between the manager's need to control the outcome and the need to engage the participants in dialogue that they perceive as worthwhile. This balance is established at the outset of any facilitation opportunity in the way the manager initiates the process.

It is useful for a manager to think of his or her relationship with a group as being similar to that of a consultant. While members of a group may be either direct reports or stakeholders from other areas of the organization, reconceptualizing them as clients puts the facilitator in the proper mind-set. Theorists in consulting process, like Peter Block, talk about a contracting phase in a consulting relationship. Block and others assert that there is a natural tendency in a consulting relationship to want to have power over the client. However, the objective is really to have power *with* the client.

The facilitator who wishes to have power over the group creates a very unstable arrangement, because group members soon realize that they are being controlled and will raise barriers that will be difficult to overcome. The best position for the facilitator to be in is to have direct and constructive impact on the group while being perceived as being at the same level.[1]

The process through which this level playing field is established is generally called *contracting*, and it is an important part of the initial phase of working with a group. The term *contract* here means an explicit agreement on what both the facilitator and the members of the group need and expect from each other and how they are going to work together. Under the best of circumstances, both the facilitator and the group enter into an agreement born of mutual consent. Much of the dialogue that takes place in the initiating phase of a facilitation relationship centers on the agreement between the facilitator and the group as to how the work will be done. To initiate and establish good working contracts, the manager acting as facilitator should be able to ask direct questions about each member's role and commitment to the task.

- Learn what the group's expectations are of a successful facilitator.
- Probe for group members' underlying concerns or risk issues that could inhibit or influence their responses negatively.
- Give direct and meaningful verbal support to positions and ideas put forth by group members.
- Be able to move from content to process in order to discuss why a particular meeting is not working effectively at any given time.

INITIATING AS BEGINNING

Initiating means beginning a new action—shifting the conversation to a different need, asking for input, and so on. A primary example of initiating takes place at the beginning of any meeting. In this situation, there are three objectives to be accomplished:

1. *Introduce* yourself, if necessary, allow others to introduce themselves, and provide an overview of the purpose of the meeting.
2. *Demonstrate* interest by establishing rapport, credibility, and trust and building a level of comfort.
3. *Orient* the participants to the meeting process and gain control of the dynamics.

The process of meeting, greeting, and gaining control is similar, regardless of the type of meeting you are facilitating. Obviously, if as the manager of the group there is a need to introduce yourself, there are bigger problems than the facilitation task at hand. There will be times when managers will be assigned to lead groups that are not part of their immediate department. These instances could be the result of being involved in cross-functional teams or task forces or groups composed of members outside of the company, such as industry groups or committees.

If a manager is not well known to the group, there is probably some defensiveness. Group members may be defensive because they fear that they will be persuaded to go in a direction they may not want to go, so the facilitator has to prove to them that he or she can be helpful and that it will be worth their while to interact openly and effectively. At the outset, the group must develop a feeling that the facilitator has a genuine interest in helping the group and has a sincere desire to incorporate the group's ideas. When a facilitator is insincere, the participants will sense it. The question that hangs in the air is, "Why should I trade my valuable time to meet with this person?"

Despite the potential for defensiveness, the best chance for developing a working relationship occurs at the beginning. The facilitator's primary objective is to present himself or herself as a person worthy of trust. A major step in overcoming defensiveness will take place if the participants have the feeling that they can depend on the facilitator to carry out a fair share of whatever tasks become part of the group results and that any information they are willing to share will be held in the strictest confidence, if necessary. It is a good idea to state at the outset the facilitator's interest in each member's ideas and concerns.

The group members also have to feel that they will have significant involvement in the recommendations or other output of the group experience. The importance of acquiring detailed information from each person in order to ensure that the recommendations or other outcomes will be mutually satisfying must be stressed.

How the group responds will depend to a great extent on how they perceive the facilitator's concern for their welfare. The empathy selected is, of course, situational. For example, if a manager is consulting with a group on a change management initiative, he or she might make empathy statements such as: "You are concerned about what will happen to your department as a result of this study, and you are confused about the different options available to you for the company's future financial needs, and it's making it difficult for you to make a decision." Naming the group's concerns shows an understanding of the emotional as well as the pragmatic side of the issue.

While empathy as a behavior does not come easily to many managers, it is a key element in successful facilitation. A very powerful tool in any interpersonal situation, the application of empathy illustrates an understanding of how the group is feeling with statements like: "We are going to work through this together, step by step, and I want you all to be sure you understand exactly what the options are before we make a decision." Good facilitators include themselves in the process by frequent use of *we*. This shows an intention to take an active part in both the analysis and the decision-making process.

Validating the Group's Assets

Successful managers see themselves as, among other things, great problem solvers. There is a natural tendency to feel that things are going to be straightened out, now that the right person has been put in charge. This view of the situation works against the manager's success with the group. When first interacting with a new group, care must be taken not to project the feeling that the group has been foolish or totally inadequate in their efforts to achieve their goals to date. Finding something positive to say about the situation will provide a strong lift to the relationship. Again, what is actually said will be based on the situation, but something like this alleviates tension: "I want you all to know that based on the circumstances as I understand them at this point, you have made significant progress in the right direction. I hope I can provide some input that will help us push through and reach our goal." There are some basic factors that lead to a favorable impression. While many of these factors are common sense, they are worth reviewing. They are:

- Be on time for appointments. If unavoidably delayed, contact the group members and provide an update or reschedule as necessary.
- Make certain that your appearance is neat and businesslike according to the standards of the organization.
- Have all your materials organized so you don't create a negative impression by having to search for the items you need.

- Your manner and conversation should be friendly but professional even with people you know well.
- If you are using computerized materials or overheads, make sure that the appropriate software is loaded and that the projector is in good working order.

BEGINNING AND INTRODUCTIONS

In one sense, the facilitator begins the meeting the moment he or she enters the room. During the informal time before "calling to order," the facilitator should make an effort to interact with each individual. Whether first or last in the room, the facilitator greets each member of the group with a smile and strong eye contact, followed by handshakes. Most often, time will be the determinant of when the meeting formally begins, but an astute facilitator will sense the appropriate moment when everyone is prepared to begin the meeting. During this process conscious inferences should be drawn about each participant. Make mental notes that can later be probed to either dispel doubts or confirm first impressions. Observation is always an important skill in managing group process. Preparing to move forward is aided by asking these questions:

- How does each person position himself or herself in relation to you? Does one person seem evasive, while another is overly friendly?
- What are the nonverbal cues among and between individuals? Do the participants all seem relaxed? Does their posture suggest receptiveness, or are there members who position themselves turned away or fold their arms as a signal that they are closed or defensive?
- How does the group arrange itself spatially? During the informal part of the meeting, do certain members gather together and exclude others? If the seating hasn't been arranged, how does everyone place himself or herself in relation to the facilitator and other members of the group?

Some time needs to be taken at the outset to allow for introductions, particularly in groups where the members are not well known to each other. The facilitator might ask each person to give a short introduction including one factor such as how they were selected for the group or what they would like to accomplish on a personal level.

Demonstrate Care and Concern

Introductions can be used to help build trust. Trust is a critical factor in the success of managing a group over time. It is a key element in your contract with the group. One way of building trust and demonstrating interest is to ask some questions. In addition to demonstrating your interest in each person, effective questioning helps them open up and talk about themselves. Initial questions must be open, friendly, and nonthreatening. Questions at this point derive naturally from what the person has included in the introduction. For example, a participant might say: "I'm Sally Smithers, and I work with John Jones in Accounting. My personal objective is to get a better handle on how we document expenses." The facilitator might follow up with: "That issue is definitely one we will be focusing on. At the right time will you share some of your thoughts on what can be done?" Facilitators may be judged initially more for the professionalism of their questions than by their expertise on the subject being considered.

These initial questions should help you engage the group through conversation that focuses on the group and their individual and collective interests. It is very important that the facilitator's interest is perceived as being sincere, rather than reaching for concerns or interests for which there is no real feeling.

Self-Disclosure

Introductions also provide opportunities for self-disclosure, which is another way of building trust. Self-disclosure is any revelation about oneself that is not readily apparent through observation or prior knowledge. Self-disclosure should not be irrelevant or too intimate. Used with care and discretion, self-disclosure can be an effective tool for establishing rapport and encouraging the exchange of information. People don't like dealing with strangers. Relevant self-disclosures encourage positive responses. This happens because when people reveal something about themselves, they appear trustworthy. Self-disclosure also encourages others to disclose information about themselves and reduces the initial defensiveness in a new group relationship. For example, let's assume that Sally responded to the earlier question by saying, "Yes, I've had several ideas, but the more I think about it, the more confusing the alternatives become." The facilitator might take this opportunity to establish a common ground through a simple disclosure. "Sally, I know what you mean. I don't work well in a vacuum. Someone once told me that when I'm talking to myself, I'm talking to a crazy person. I believe that being able to bounce ideas off of the people here, you'll get some perspective."

The expression of interest and concern may be a distinctly separate element or integrated with the introductions. It can range from nonrelated personal comments to addressing the specific reason for the meeting. The purpose is to indicate an interest in each group member as a person as well as a client or colleague. When interest and concern have been exchanged, everyone will be more at ease and motivated to exchange information. Expressions of interest and concern are great trust builders. Trust is the most important component for stimulating the free flow of truthful information.

After your conversation starters develop an initial rapport, you are ready to set the stage for the rest of the meeting. The most successful facilitators view the meeting as a means by which both the leader and the group members can accomplish certain goals. To do this (in addition to being clear about what needs to be accomplished in the meeting) facilitators need to learn what each person wants from the meeting, too. One very successful facilitator says that she begins every meeting with the same question: "Why did you agree to meet with me today?" This question, and others like it, may enable each group member to spell out his or her primary objectives and concerns. Here are some things to remember about demonstrating interest and concern:

- You have about four minutes to create a good or bad first impression.
- Three questions must be answered to the group's satisfaction:
  1. Do you have credibility?
  2. Do you care about us?
  3. Can we trust you?
- Many meetings succeed or fail based upon the personal relationship with the facilitator.
- You are always selling yourself first, then your ideas and solutions.

Orient the Group

Orientation establishes the parameters of the meeting. It clarifies for the group what will occur. It is easy to make the assumption that the members of a group or meeting attendees have a clear idea of what the meeting is about. It is amazing how often this is not the case. Even with sincere attempts at informing people beforehand, memos and e-mails are often overlooked or not attended to carefully because of workload, priorities, or other factors so common in today's workplace. Every facilitation event should begin with a thorough orientation.

Orientation is the first major step in taking control of the interaction. It answers these questions:

1. What do we need to do?
2. How long will it take?
3. Will it obligate me?

Here are some key points for orientation:

- Properly orienting the group at each and every meeting lets you set the stage for discovering the necessary facts and feelings and the level of commitment in the group.
- Knowing what is going to happen helps put your group at ease and gets them involved in discussing their issues and how to resolve them.
- Orientation lets you establish yourself as a person who is concerned with the group's needs, their wants, and their time.

Initiating Throughout the Meeting Process

The behavior of initiating is not confined to the beginning of a meeting. There are many points during your interaction with the group where you will call upon your initiating skill to support and enhance the relationship-building process.

Here are some additional situations that require initiating:

- asking for new ideas
- focusing attention on an additional need or problem
- monitoring individual follow-up

When initiating a new subject or a new direction for the group to follow, skilled facilitators develop the habit of initiating these shifts by using benefit statements. A benefit statement provides a reason for moving in the direction that the facilitator wants to go. It makes transitions less abrupt and in effect reasserts the contract developed between the facilitator and group members and gains their assent to move in the desired direction. An effective benefit statement accomplishes two things:

1. It makes the connection between achieving the group's goals and objectives and the necessity for the group to engage in discussing this particular issue.
2. Where appropriate, it establishes the benefit accrued directly to individuals in the group by engaging in this part of the discussion.

Following is an example of a benefit statement that moves the group to a new issue: "We have put a lot of ideas on the table about what needs to be done to move forward with the redesign of our two key products. I think at this point we need to focus our attention on gaining an accurate understanding of our financial resources so that we can meet our goals." It is then a good idea to gain verbal approval from the group to move on to the new issue.

Benefit statements accomplish several things.

- They prevent group members from objecting to the introduction of the new subject.
- They enable group members to feel as if they are participating in the process.
- They tend to make group members feel more comfortable engaging in discussion of the new issue.
- They help prevent group members from feeling manipulated.
- They make the facilitator feel more comfortable moving on to a new subject area.
- They aid in the continued building of rapport and trust and orient the group to the facilitator's ongoing expectations.

Initiating is the stage in the process that establishes rapport, direction, control, credibility, and trust. All these things are extraordinarily important if a manager is going to be perceived as a strong leader. Managers who work effectively as facilitators develop solid working relationships with direct reports and others in the organization. They are seen as people who are committed to sharing information with others and go beyond communicating only what is necessary. They succeed in developing a climate in which all members of the team share information openly and focus their energies on achieving the overall goals and objectives rather than individual agendas.

NOTE

1. Peter Block, *Flawless Consulting: A Guide to Getting Your Expertise Used* (San Diego, CA: University Associates, 1981), 41.

CHAPTER 6

Questioning to Stimulate and Control Discussion

We begin the discussion of questioning with a basic question of our own: Who is the person in control, the one asking questions or the one doing the talking? Some people when asked this question respond that the person talking is in control because they have the floor and are presenting their opinions and ideas. However, just the opposite is true. The person in control of any interpersonal interaction is the one who controls the dynamics, that is, the direction and content that is being exchanged during the process. The person asking questions is in control because he or she is eliciting responses from others and managing the discussion without doing so overtly. Gaining and maintaining control is the power of questioning.

The question may be the most important tool in the facilitator's toolbox. The best facilitators are those who ask questions rather than make presentations—those who listen more than they talk. Questioning is a powerful tool because it involves the group in the process of discovering their own needs and solutions. Questions are your means of controlling the dynamics because questions have a very powerful influence on behavior and thought process.

KEY CONCEPTS

- Understanding the importance of asking questions.
- Recognizing the need for and creating open questions.
- Recognizing the need for and creating closed questions.

- Recognizing the need for and creating probing questions.
- Formulating questions to stimulate both factual and feeling information.
- Defining question categories.

Questioning involves the group in creating a solution, which in turn helps raise the level of commitment. Effective group members are open, candid, and involved in the process. Getting this kind of involvement, and getting it early in the meeting, takes skill and the ability to frame good questions.

Anytime a question is asked, the most likely response by far is some kind of answer.

"What time is it?"

"Twelve o'clock."

"What day next week would be best for our next meeting?"

"Tuesday."

Sometimes a group member will answer a question with another question. It is easy to take control of the conversation by responding to a question with a question. We will discuss more about responding in Chapter 8. However, a rule of thumb suggests that if a facilitator answers two questions in a row without counteracting with a question, he or she has lost control of the meeting. The way a question is worded can significantly influence the response received, the completeness of the answer provided, and the impact the question has in terms of creating credibility and trust.

Questions will help you

- gain important information
- control the interaction
- determine specific needs
- create a better understanding of the situation
- increase the perception of trust and credibility
- increase the probability of obtaining a commitment

Managers who facilitate bring a lot of baggage with them. Because they have experience, opinions of their own, and ultimate accountability, they are tempted to rely on assumptions. If questions are not used effectively, these assumptions are not adequately tested. Making assumptions is a dangerous strategy and often causes the facilitator to go off in directions inappropriate for the group or creates additional obstacles to overcome. Questions can be either open or closed. Open questions get the widest, richest range of responses. Closed questions require a yes or no, up or down answer.

FRAMING QUESTIONS

Many facilitators make a serious mistake at the outset of the discussion. We have already discussed that one of the important outcomes of group process is to leave the group with a sense of accomplishment. Unless people feel they are getting somewhere, their interest and enthusiasm soon diminish. A major role of the facilitator is to present the discussion topic to the group in such a way that everyone feels an opportunity to participate and express their ideas. The use of an appropriate question plays an important role in getting the discussion going in the right direction.

Questions for discussion need to be phrased as neutral. They should not incorporate a suggested solution. Consider the following question: "How high should we raise salaries in order to keep our engineers from leaving the company?" The underlying issue suggested in this question is that the level of turnover among engineers is problematic. A question of this scope may require information-gathering, problem-solving, and decision-making activities. However, the way the question is phrased suggests that a solution has already been reached. Someone (most probably the manager conducting the meeting) has determined, either unilaterally or by some other means, that the solution to the problem is to raise salaries. The only question offered to the group involves determining by how much the salaries will be raised. Phrasing a question in this manner eliminates the potential for alternative solutions. There may be members of the group that feel that salaries are not the issue— or, at least, not the only issue. Because of the way the question is phrased, those individuals will be reluctant to offer their thoughts and ideas about the problem. Engineers could be seeking alternative employment for many reasons including such things as lack of resources, working conditions, inadequate or antiquated equipment, or feeling unappreciated for their efforts. By incorporating the statement of the solution in the discussion question, the facilitator may miss an opportunity to develop a much more comprehensive, and thereby more successful, solution to the problem.

Consider phrasing the question this way: "What can we do to impact turnover among the engineers?" The response and subsequent discussion around this issue could of course include salary range. However, it does not suggest that the manager who is facilitating the meeting has already made important decisions about the components of the solution.

A similar problem occurs when the group is provided with a discussion question that appears to offer only two alternatives. The following question demonstrates this problem. "Should we lower the price of our products to gain additional market share?" In addition to containing a suggested solution, "lower the price of our products," the question seems to require a yes or no response. Questions of this type tend to split the group into competing factions and to make an impartial exploration of the problem very difficult. If there are strong opinions on both sides of the issue, what inevitably happens is that the discussion rapidly becomes a debate.

OPEN QUESTIONS

Open questions are questions that seek the group's opinions, feelings, plans, strategies, ideas, and the like, on a variety of pertinent subjects. They uncover and help the group recognize and acknowledge needs, problems, and opportunities. Responding to open questions involves the group more directly in the process. People generally like to talk about themselves, and the more a person has a chance to talk, explain, agree, or disagree during the discussion, the more ownership he or she will feel toward the final outcome.

A facilitator has at his or her command several options with regard to the type of questions to ask. Question type is usually determined by the intent of the question. If the facilitator is looking for a broad spectrum of response, he or she will select open questions. While the open question is often thought of as more difficult from a control perspective, it actually has a very strong control dimension. Although the open question calls for a broader response, it contains that response within a defined area outlined by the question.

Almost all discussions and training centering around interpersonal issues involve some discussion of open questions. Almost every manager who would aspire to become an excellent facilitator has been exposed to the notion of open questions somewhere in his or her academic or professional career. That said, I have demonstrated time and again that while most people understand what open questions are conceptually, when they are asked to produce one or more, particularly in live interactive environments, they are unable to do so. I have conducted simple exercises during training sessions that required participants to write on a piece of paper three questions on any subject. It is the rare instance when any of the questions written by the entire group fall into the open mode. Using open questions is less natural to most people than the closed question. This is the result of the language development process that begins at birth. Parents are most likely to frame questions to children in nonopen ways, such as:

- "Are you hungry?"
- "Did you brush your teeth?"
- "Do you want to go to the movies?"

Rarely will a parent sitting across the table from a young child at the end of a meal ask something like: "Tell me how you felt about dinner tonight." The "closed-question syndrome" is reinforced by the children themselves, who tend to be secretive. Their early years are spent carefully guarding an internal privacy since most external privacy is denied to them. Therefore, they do not readily respond to open questions.

Facilitators managing group process effectively make a conscious effort to frame questions in the open mode, particularly at the beginning of a meeting. It is very useful and highly recommended that a list of open questions be prepared in advance, rather than depending on being able to generate an open question at the moment.

Open questions encourage people to talk more freely about their needs and to provide important information about their motives and processes. Open questions always begin with expansive questioning words like: *what*, *why*, and *how*. They may also be constructed as statements, using phrases like "Tell me," "Let's talk about," or "Help me understand." The difficulty most people have with open questions is not using enough of them. Insightful open questions can be great conversation starters, and the right open questions can do a great deal to improve the facilitator's credibility.

One way of developing a useful list of open questions is to use the PAGO principle. Plan questions that cover information about the

- *people* (questions about the group members or people related to the group's mission)
- *actions* (questions about the current activities)
- *goals* (questions about what the group or company is trying to accomplish)
- *obstacles* (questions about problems the group or company is having in meeting its goals)

Not all people are comfortable with open questions. If a group member has some conflict or emotional involvement with a particular subject area or is suspicious of the facilitator's motive for the question, the response will not be extensive. Hostility or suspicion can be determined immediately through the response. The response will usually take the form of a question that forces the facilitator to be more specific. Here are a couple of examples.

Larry: "How are you doing?"

Mary: "What have you heard?"

Harry: "Tell me about your plans."

Terry: "What do you want to know?"

There are a limited number of ways to phrase an open question. Question words like *what* and *how* call for open responses.

- "What planning has been done so far?"
- "What are some of the problems we'll have in finding new customers?"
- "How will we cover the costs of additional personnel?"
- "How do you all feel about the progress being made developing the new product?"

Open questions can also be initiated by phrases that call for an expanded response. These often take the form of statements.

- "Let's talk about some of the major financial concerns."
- "Help me understand the thinking behind changing the delivery schedule."

Some points to remember about open questions:

- The relationship with the group can be enhanced if the right questions are asked by the facilitator.
- Open questions seek the opinions, feelings, plans, strategies, and ideas on a variety of pertinent subjects.
- Open questions can serve as very effective ways of demonstrating and enhancing your credibility with your group.
- When asking open questions, a facilitator must take care not to respond before the questioning process is done. The most critical issues tend to surface at the end of the discussion.

CLOSED QUESTIONS

Closed questions can often be answered with a simple yes or no or with particular facts that are important to the situation. These are questions that direct the group to respond with a specific answer. You can also provide a limited choice of alternatives from which the group can choose. Closed questioning can be more efficient than open questioning at gaining specific information. This is particularly true if the primary purpose of the meeting is fact finding. By limiting the range of choices, you can cover several fact-finding issues in a relatively short time.

Closed questions are very useful for verifying and confirming specific information obtained as a result of open questions. They can also be used to provide direction and set the stage for additional open questions to expand the value and meaning of the facts uncovered. They may also be used to confirm agreement to proceed or acceptance of a suggestion that you may have made. Because of the narrow response range, there is a limited amount of information that you can obtain by using a closed question.

Asking closed questions comes more naturally to most people and has important usage. A short sequence of focused questions can orient the group to important things to think about, but some facilitators overuse them and find themselves interrogating the group rather than having a natural conversation. This is a particular caution for managers.

Closed questions are used when it is important to focus the group on a specific area of interest. Closed questions involve more than the request for a data point or a simple yes or no answer. There is a large middle ground that may be phrased in a closed manner but still entices an open response. The wording, intonation, and nonverbal behavior used create a need for the group to answer more broadly.

- "What do you think is our greatest opportunity in this market?"
- "Who will exert the most influence on the success of our project?"
- "Do we have the right people in the right jobs?"

Other questions are distinctly closed in form and intent. In this way the facilitator limits the range of responses available to the group.

- "Do we want to take on this responsibility?"
- "Which side are we going to support on this issue?"
- "Who can make the meeting on Thursday?"
- "Would you say we are budgeting too high, too low, or just right?"

Here are some things to remember about closed questions:

- They are effective for getting specific factual information.
- Answers to closed questions are easy to systematize and analyze.
- As long as they relate to nonpersonal things, they are generally perceived as easy to answer.
- They are useful to clarify and confirm information derived from open questions.
- Where self-disclosure is required, they can be perceived as more threatening than open questions.

PROBING QUESTIONS

Probing questions help to clarify misunderstanding, uncover objections, and focus the group's interests and concerns. Probes are the facilitator's refining tool. Like archaeologists on a search for hidden treasure, probes remove layers of material in order to arrive at the essential information. In one sense of the word, all questions "probe." However, in this context, probing is a follow-up to an original question. It grows out of a felt need for more information—a feeling on the part of the facilitator that the answers generated from the initial question did not provide the full or correct response needed. Probes must suit the occasion. There are two basic types: *direct* and *neutral*.

Direct probes are simply questions that require a fuller response:

- "What do you mean by . . . ?"
- "Could you go into that more?"
- "You must have a good reason for making . . ."
- "Can you help me understand?"
- "What happened then?"
- "How did that happen?"

Neutral probes lead the group toward a fuller response. You are communicating that you are interested in additional information.

- "I see."
- "Really?"
- "Uh-huh."
- "Hmmm."
- "And . . . ?"
- (Silence)

One characteristic that distinguishes the skillful facilitator from the novice is the level of comfort with silence. Many people feel the need to fill every moment with noise, appropriate or otherwise. Almost everyone has experienced moments in both formal and social situations when there is a prolonged silence among a group of people. The feeling of wanting to say something to bridge the silence is palpable. When applied purposefully, silence is one of the best probing techniques. You can use the universal need to fill silence with words to encourage group members to provide more information. Simply leave silent space that they may be compelled to fill with additional information.

The use of silence is enhanced by appropriately applying a wide range of nonverbal behavior. A smile, a frown, a nod of the head, a raised eyebrow, and the like, communicate expectations for more information and will usually elicit a response from most groups.

Here are some things to remember about probing questions:

- They can be framed as either open or closed questions.
- They are used to dig deeper into a subject area, rather than to open a new area.
- Too many direct probes in a sequence will appear threatening.
- The use of probes grows out of a felt need on your part for more information.
- Use a variety of probes so that you don't sound repetitious or superficial.

QUESTION CATEGORIES

In addition to different types of questions (open, closed, probe), questions can also be classified in various categories: *hypothetical* questions, *analytical* questions, and *reactive* questions. These question categories cross over the various types. For example, hypothetical questions can be both open and closed. They are also very effective as probes. The same can be said for both analytical and reactive questions.

Hypothetical Questions

Hypothetical questions place group members in the context of a particular problem or a potential solution. Hypothetical questions begin with phrases like, "What if we . . ."; "Let's assume that . . ."; "You're a customer looking at our Web site . . ."; "What would we do in the case of . . ." Hypothetical questions are particularly effective at focusing the group on practicalities. It is one thing to talk about the "customer" in the abstract sense and quite another to picture a particular customer reacting and responding to products and service levels within a particular context. Individual group members' responses to hypothetical questions also provide insights into the problem-solving approaches and management styles of people in the group. They also tend to draw out information from group members that they might not ordinarily give. One of the primary roles of the facilitator particularly in problem-solving discussions is to play devil's advocate. "What if" hypothetical questions help the group to collectively deal with many contingencies and potential problems that might not surface without going through this exercise.

The technology group at one major electronic financial trading network continually went through hypothetical exercises prior to the disastrous events that took place on September 11, 2001. Working as groups, they consistently grappled with questions like, "What if there is a major outage in one of the primary data centers?" "What if trans-Atlantic lines go down?" "What if major problems occur late at night when key personnel are difficult to assemble?" As a result, even though all of the above suggested scenarios occurred at essentially the same time, the network was restored and 95 percent operable by the following day.

Analytical Questions

Analytical questions cause the group to look at issues critically and to evaluate various options that may be available. For example, one of the key factors in problem-solving discussions is the development of criteria against which potential solutions can be measured. At a critical juncture in the discussion when solutions are being selected or crafted among the various options, it is the facilitator's job to keep the group focused on the criteria they established earlier on. Questions like, "How do these two approaches differ?" or "What do we see as the advantages and disadvantages of moving in this direction?" help keep the focus. It is also useful in many situations for the facilitator to use a flip chart, white board, or other visual medium to develop a decision matrix. One of the difficulties of keeping a group on an analytical track is that members of the group may be emotionally invested in certain approaches or solutions that blind them to some of the practicalities. When the group environment is emotionally charged, a successful facilitator may achieve a consensus by turning the discussion away from the various solutions and focusing on the criteria. If the group can be brought to consensus about the criteria and the weighting of the criteria, they are more likely to get past the emotional blockages keeping them from making the best choices.

Reactive Questions

A reactive question is like a hypothetical question posed after the fact. It is designed to elicit responses about events that have already occurred. The purpose is to focus the group on evaluating past situations in order to make more effective applications to the future. Although the discussion may engage in some comparison as well as contrasting observations, they differ from analytical questions in that they are not asking the group to measure or select from among variables. When a facilitator uses reactive questions, he or she is soliciting the group's opinions and feelings on events that have happened and the subsequent results of those events. Questions like, "How did you feel about combining both sales organizations immediately after the merger?" or "What do you think caused the drop in sales last month?" provide opportunities for group members to present their ideas and theories. When using reactive questions, the facilitator needs to be prepared to control the potential for argument, blaming, and other aggressive behavior. In response to the question about the fall-off in sales, there is the potential for someone in the group to offer the opinion that the resulting loss in sales revenue was due to the fact that the salespeople were simply not doing their job. If there are salespeople in the group, the ensuing discussion could be very lively. When a facilitator uses reactive questions, he or she must also be prepared to follow up with hypothetical and analytical questions that refocus the group on the issues and away from unproductive finger pointing.

The overall success of a discussion depends a great deal on the facilitator's capacity for rapid analysis. This is especially true when managers facilitate. The manager must be able to see in what direction the group is turning to catch significant points even when they are encompassed in detail, to discover agreements between various points of view, and to strip controversial issues of unnecessary complexity. The manager as facilitator must be able and prepared to state the results of his or her analysis of the situation clearly and briefly and to make the essential points stand out before the group as vividly as they do in his or her own mind. Particular care must be taken by the manager to project the quality of fairness and impartiality. Special efforts must be made to ensure that minority views are allowed expression. This is done through the effective phrasing of questions and summarizing the contributions of each of the members fairly. This focus on fairness and impartiality helps maintain the spirit of cooperative inquiry among people who have different points of view. Self-control is paramount. Leadership in this context must be tempered with tact both in words and in manner. In the role of facilitator there is no place for a leader who is easily irritated or says things in a way that irritates others. A good rule to follow is always to accept comments and state them with the most generous interpretation possible.

We have put much emphasis on questioning as an extremely important tool leading to the success of group process. Good questioning does not happen automatically and on the spur of the moment. For most of us the ability to use questions effectively derives from careful preparation. Knowing and analyzing the subject as well as the people in the group will help the facilitator prepare key questions that uncover issues, motivate group members to participate, and develop an atmosphere of cooperation and trust.

CHAPTER 7

Active Listening

If getting the group to tell you what you need to know is your first priority, listening to what is said must have equal weight. Listening is more than hearing. It's a skill that must be and can be developed. The process requires concentration, analysis, and feedback. Active listening makes the group feel that the facilitator understands their needs and understands them as people.

KEY CONCEPTS

- Active listening behaviors.
- Identifying and using the four types of active listening (acknowledging, sympathizing, paraphrasing, and empathizing).
- Overcoming the barriers to active listening.

Active listening not only helps focus attention on what the group is saying; it can often go a long way to help the group solve problems. Actively listening tells the group that you are interested in understanding what they have to say—that you care about them. And amazingly enough, simply feeding back people's ideas often helps them sort out and come to solutions and conclusions that you would like them to discover.

Effective listening is difficult under the best of conditions. However, the difficulty is compounded in the group situation because a facilitator needs to listen to a variety of points of view being presented by individuals who differ in the way they present their ideas. The situation is made more complex when it is the manager who is facilitating. I have discovered over the years that managers as a class are not necessarily good listeners. But when the manager is effective as a facilitator, there is more power in listening and absorbing than there is in presenting one's own ideas to the group. Being a good listener is a difficult task. The listener must make a concerted effort to understand what is being said, retain information over protracted periods of time in order to develop a synthesis, and make judgments by filtering the information based on personal standards of taste and discrimination. Individuals differ in their ability to listen effectively. In the same way, they might differ in their ability to read or to do any other activity. However, barring an organic dysfunction, listening ability can be improved through focusing attention on its importance and practicing good listening behaviors.

WHAT IS ACTIVE LISTENING?

The term *active listening* has become fairly commonplace when discussing communication dynamics. At the simplest level, it points to the fact that good listening is not merely a passive soaking up of the speaker's words or arguments; rather it is an active effort to derive meaning from all aspects of the communication situation—from the speaker's tone of voice, movements, gestures, and facial expressions as well as from the words. In addition, active listening includes interpretation and appraisal, a constant and critical consideration of the ideas presented, the materials by which these ideas are supported or explained, the purposes that motivate them, and the language in which they are expressed. In addition to the active internal listening behaviors described above, an effective listener also manifests external behaviors that both project that listening is taking place and encourage further discussion and amplification.

Language, the Imperfect Tool

Language is a wonderful tool, but it has its limitations. One basic limitation that impacts on listening is the fact that the meaning of words lies within people rather than in the words themselves. This factor creates many opportunities for "bypassing." Bypassing is a communication

dynamic that occurs when two or more people have a different understanding of the same word. Most of us can hardly get through a single
day without having at least one example of bypassing. However, consider the following passage from *Alice in Wonderland*. The Mouse is
speaking to the Duck and he says,

" ' . . . the patriotic archbishop of Canterbury, found it advis-
able—' "

"Found *what?*" said the Duck.

"Found *it*," the Mouse replied rather crossly: "of course you know
what 'it' means."

"I know what 'it' means well enough, when *I* find a thing," said the
Duck: "it's generally a frog or a worm. The question is, what did the
archbishop find?"[1]

Because bypassing is so prevalent in all of our communication interactions, a primary listening behavior for any facilitator is clarifying
and confirming. Over many years of analyzing and diagnosing group
interaction problems, I have noted that many groups that have difficulty
achieving success have not effectively defined everyone's perception
of the key issues involved in the discussion. The facilitator's job as an
active listener is to continually clarify and confirm his or her understanding of what is being said and thereby surface any discrepancies
in the perception of others on the same issue. It is not always necessary
for everyone in the group to agree on a particular definition, but in
order for communication to take place, everyone in the group needs to
understand what other members of the group mean when they use a
term and how they are interpreting a particular term when it is put out
as part of the discussion.

Projecting Objectivity

Professional facilitators often come from outside the organization and
are truly objective in their approach to the problem and issues since
they are not burdened by the constraints of organizational politics, positional power, or economic outcomes. Managers who facilitate, however, generally do have points of view on the matters at hand that are
being discussed. They often have a preferred solution that on some
level they would like to sell to the group. Good listening behavior does
not allow this point of view to affect the objectivity and emotional
neutrality that should be preserved throughout the listening experience.

A key behavior in projecting objectivity and neutrality is the withholding of evaluation until later stages of the discussion. In this way, listening does not become an exercise in fault finding by seeking out and constantly commenting on the weak points in the various ideas and arguments being put forth. Admittedly, a difficult mind-set to maintain, a successful manager acting as a facilitator listens critically but also sympathetically and tries to derive the greatest possible benefit from the ideas being offered by each group member.

Facilitators from outside the organization focus almost exclusively on process. That is, they try to ensure that the functional aspects of the group dynamic are optimized. They provide structure, help define the issues and terms, mediate disputes, coordinate ideas, motivate participation, and synthesize results. Managers within the organization who engage in facilitation activities are also charged with the responsibility of accomplishing the same objectives. However, their task is made more difficult because they are often saddled with the execution of the results of their facilitation efforts. For managers, effective listening means more than learning new facts or understanding more clearly the positions and ideas of the people in the group. Managers need to make judgments or evaluations of the ideas being presented. They must analyze critically not only the ideas themselves but also the evidence and reasoning by which they are supported. They have to separate those appeals that are logical or fact-based from those that are primarily emotional and must be able to look beneath the flourishes of style or expression to consider the intrinsic worth of each speaker's point of view.

Guides to Effective Listening

Like many other things, becoming an effective listener requires a combination of self-evaluation and practice. Below are some guidelines that facilitators can use to listen for both comprehension and evaluation.

1. *Identify a speaker's major or leading ideas and concentrate closely on each as it is expressed.* Take care to identify each major idea as it is stated and separate it from the developmental material that is associated with it. This can be challenging since most ideas put forth in a group setting have elements of spontaneity that do not always lend themselves to a structured presentation.

2. *Identify the structure or pattern of organization that the speaker employs.* Does the speaker tend to order the material according to time, space, or other classifications? Members of the group may use different forms of ordering material as a style preference. It is possible for two people to be in nearly complete agreement on a particular point but not recognize it because they are organizing and presenting the material in differing ways.

3. *Focus on the details that support or develop the major ideas.* Does the speaker use illustrations or examples to support his or her main thesis? Are any of the facts or data being presented new information that was not previously known?

4. *Filter the opinions and ideas being presented through your own previous experience and knowledge.* While most managers will do this intuitively, by focusing attention on the need to make these comparisons, the listening process becomes more of an active effort. How does what is being said fit into the context of what is already known? Does this information or idea refine, add to, or qualify previous knowledge? How can the new ideas be integrated into a previously held understanding of the issues or problems being discussed?

5. *Evaluate the speaker's analysis of the problem.* Has the speaker recognized all aspects or facets of the problem? Has he or she correctly judged the scope and importance of each? Is what is being proposed practical and desirable as a method of meeting the problem?

6. *Evaluate the speaker's reasoning.* Is the reasoning sound? Does it contain flaws or fallacies? Are there generalizations that are unsupported? Are causes or issues put on the table that really don't relate to the current problem? Do the examples or analogies seem fair or pertinent to the discussion?

7. *Evaluate the evidence.* Does the speaker base his or her views upon facts, or does the presentation include unsupported assertions backed only by colorful phrases and a positive or aggressive manner of delivery? When facts are presented, are they presented fairly, or is there a clear bias?

8. *Evaluate the speaker's emotional appeals.* Highly motivated and enthusiastic individuals can often sell an idea based almost purely on the notion that they feel more strongly than anyone else in the room about moving in a particular direction. Do the emotional appeals cover up for a lack of sound reasoning? Are the ideas presented and developed with restraint and good taste? Does the emotion grow out of a true deep feeling about the issue and general conviction, or is there a sense of opportunism?

9. *Evaluate the speaker's use of language.* Are the presentation aspects taking precedence over the ideas? Are visuals and colorful language being used to do the work that should be done by facts and figures? Do the recommen-

dations seem so general that they could mean almost anything? Does the speaker use buzzwords, loaded words, or name-calling in order to emphasize points?

BARRIERS TO LISTENING

In addition to the skills needed to be an effective listener, there are several factors both within ourselves and in the environment that inhibit the facilitator's ability to listen well.

Here are some things that get in the way of being a good listener:

- the tendency to concentrate most of our attention on making connections between what is being said and what we already believe
- the tendency to judge or evaluate the content of what a group member is saying before fully understanding what we have heard
- the tendency to jump to conclusions—hearing what we want to hear
- the tendency to interpret words and phrases differently than the speaker intended—bypassing
- the tendency to interrupt—preferring to hear our own voice over another's
- fear that we might have to admit we are wrong in what we assumed to be true
- the tendency to feel we know more about what the group needs than the group itself

As stated at the beginning of this chapter, it often appears that we have more to gain by talking than by listening. One big advantage of talking is that it gives you a chance to convince others of your point of view. In many business situations, it appears that the key to success is the ability to speak well. This approach to dealing with business issues becomes ingrained and applied to all business-related situations.

Talking also gives a person the chance to release energy in a way that listening can't. When someone is frustrated, the chance to talk can often help them feel better.

Talking provides a person with a chance to gain attention and admiration. Tell jokes, and everyone will think you are funny. Offer advice, and they will be grateful for your help. Tell them what you know, and they will be impressed by your wisdom.

While it is true that talking does have many advantages, it is important to realize that listening pays big dividends in facilitating. Listening provides a measure of control perhaps even greater than talking, since active listening demonstrates your willingness to hear others' concerns and leaves them open to thinking about your ideas and solutions. Listening is often reciprocal. You get what you give.

THE ELEMENTS AND LEVELS OF GOOD LISTENING

Becoming a more effective listener is more than a matter of just trying harder. It helps to begin with a basic understanding of listening as a construct and how it operates in our lives. Most of us who do not live either in a jungle or in the white-out conditions of the arctic north spend most of our waking activity in a visual world of three dimensions. Visual confirmation takes precedence over our auditory experience.

In their provocative article on acoustic space, Edmund Carpenter and Marshall McLuhan raise important distinctions between seeing and hearing. Most of us consider that our visual experience is simply a product of physiology. Carpenter and McLuhan illustrate that it is a learned activity.

It is therefore worth recalling that the child must learn to see the world as we know it. At or shortly after birth, his eyes are as perfectly developed as a camera mechanism as they will ever be. In a sense they are too perfect and too mechanical, since they present him with a world in which everything is inverted, doubled, laterally reversed, and devoid of depth. In the course of time by a tremendous tour de force of learning, he turns the world right side up, achieves binocular fusion, and reverses the lateral field so that he now sees his father as one person, erect, whole, and bilaterally oriented.[2]

Speaking further about vision, they go on to point out that people tend to see selectively. That is, they suppress or ignore much of the visual stimuli in order to locate and identify specific objects. As a contrast to vision, however, auditory space has no point of focus. While the eye focuses pinpoints, abstracts, locating each object in physical space against a background, the ear receives sound from any direction. As a result, listening as a skill is harder to focus. As with vision, we learn over time to be selective in what we hear.

To develop our listening ability, we need to make conscious decisions about the level of attention and the amount of effort we put into each listening experience. To make it accessible, we break listening down into four elements. These elements represent a hierarchy of listening behaviors.

There are four *elements* of good listening:

1. *attention*—the focused perception of both visual and verbal stimuli
2. *hearing*—the physiological act of "opening the gates to your ears"
3. *understanding*—assigning meaning to the messages received
4. *remembering*—the storing of meaningful information

In addition to the four elements, there are also four levels of listening: acknowledging, sympathizing, paraphrasing, and empathizing. The four levels of listening range from passive to interactive when considered separately. However, the most effective listeners are able to project all four levels at the same time. That is, they demonstrate that they are paying attention and making an effort to understand and evaluate what it is they are hearing, and they complete the process by demonstrating through their responses their level of comprehension and interest in what the speaker is saying.

We will focus on level four—reactive listening or mirroring—because it represents listening at the highest level, and to do it effectively, it can be assumed that the facilitator has employed the previous three levels.

THE FOUR TYPES OF MIRRORING

Much that is required for becoming a good listener happens internally. However, there are also external manifestations of active listening that communicate to the group that a sincere effort to listen on the part of the facilitator is taking place. We call these *mirroring behaviors* because they feed back to the speaker observable data that show listening taking place. These mirroring behaviors can be divided into four types: acknowledging, sympathizing, paraphrasing, and empathizing.

Acknowledging

At the lowest level of mirroring, we demonstrate that we are paying attention. This is done by acknowledging.

Acknowledging

- demonstrates two of the four elements of good listening—attention and hearing
- is the simplest of all forms of active listening
- can be done by verbal or nonverbal signs, which also function as prompts for additional information
- is a direct way to let the group know you are listening and receiving its message
- demonstrates interest and encourages the flow of information from the group to you

Verbal and nonverbal acknowledging behavior says to the group, "I'm listening. I might not agree or accept your point of view, but I care about what you're saying and I'm aware of what's going on."

It is very difficult to continuously attend to what another person is saying. At one time or another we all lose track, especially in lengthy conversations. There is nothing abnormal about that. Our ability to concentrate for a prolonged period of time is limited.

When the facilitator finds himself or herself tuning out, there is no reason to fake it and pretend that he or she was listening. This comes across to the group as phony and creates a barrier for rapport, trust, and relationship-building. The facilitator should say something like, "Please go over that again, so I fully understand it." That kind of response usually elicits positive reactions from the other person, because it reaffirms a commitment to listening as carefully as possible.

Acknowledging also means avoiding becoming involved in some nonrelated activity while someone else is talking. Many people feel that if the listener is fiddling with paper clips, shuffling papers, or looking over notes, he or she is disinterested, even if that is not the case. Few people believe that a person can listen to what is being said and at the same time concentrate on some unrelated activity. Group members tend to believe that the facilitator's attention has to be either on them or on the activity but not both, especially when what they are saying is important to them and when they want the facilitator to be listening fully.

The facilitator's face is important, too. Maintain natural and consistent eye contact with someone. One's posture may be relaxed, and the body attentive, but a facilitator's facial expression may say, "I'm not interested." People generally assume that when a person is excited, in doubt, in deep thought, or interested, his or her face shows it. Consequently, when there seems to be almost no muscle movement in a person's face, people will probably interpret that as a lack of feeling.

One sure way that a facilitator can let the group know that he or she is paying attention is through eye contact. Reasonably consistent and natural eye contact is a sign of recognition and acknowledgment. It says in effect, "I'm tuned in—I hear you."

Your posture and the movements of your body can also affect a person's perception of you as a listener. If you are in continual motion, tapping a foot, fiddling with a pencil or paper clip, drumming your fingers, and so on, your group members may get the impression that you are anxious to get on with it, and they may interpret that as pressure. If, on the other hand, you focus on them and nod affirmatively, people generally see that as acknowledgment. Some experts suggest that having both soles of your feet on the floor, your hands on the table, and leaning slightly forward all contribute to a good businesslike posture.

Finally, facilitators can listen to acknowledge by using neutral probes—noises that indicate the facilitator is keeping up with what the other person is saying and is interested in having him or her continue.

Examples

• The head may be nodded.
• "I see."
• "Yes, go on."
• "Ah hah . . ."
• "Okay."
• "And then?"

Sympathizing

The next level of active listening is sympathizing. Sympathy is not always an appropriate response. It denotes a lack of objectivity or, in some cases, it may appear as if the facilitator is taking sides. For some situations, however, sympathy can play a powerful role in connecting the facilitator with the group or issue and enhance the building of trust.

Sympathizing

- demonstrates three elements of good listening: attention, hearing, and understanding
- acknowledges that what the group has said has had an effect on the facilitator
- reveals *the facilitator's* feelings about what he or she has heard
- can run the gamut from pity and charity to sincere compassion for the speaker's experience

Sympathizing can be a very helpful tool in the process of fact finding. Group members will be more willing to discuss sensitive issues if they feel that the facilitator is providing a "sympathetic ear." In the following examples, notice that the words *I* and *me* focus on the facilitator rather than the group member.

Examples

- "I am very sorry that happened to you."
- "I understand your concern."
- "That same thing happened to me, and I know what you're experiencing."
- "I can appreciate why you are resistant to the idea of committing a set amount of money to new equipment if the business isn't there."

Paraphrasing

Effective paraphrasing is a more complex response than acknowledging or sympathizing. Not only must the listener pay attention or phrase a response about his or her feelings, but the paraphrase must demonstrate a command of the content the speaker has provided and that the content has been mentally processed by the facilitator. Paraphrasing means listening carefully to the individual's words and then restating, in your own words, your understanding of what has been said. It is an important skill that takes practice and patience.

Paraphrasing

- demonstrates all four elements of good listening: attention, hearing, under-standing, and remembering
- tells the speaker that the words he or she has said have been thought through in some manner and committed to memory
- gives the speaker the opportunity to correct, clarify, or amplify the facilita-tor's understanding if, for some reason, he or she has misunderstood what has been said
- allows the facilitator to serve as a verbal sounding board
- does not imply approval or disapproval of what an individual has said

Examples

- "So what you're saying is that the cost of materials rose sharply, and you got caught a little short."
- "If I understand you correctly, you would be interested in seeing some ideas that could help you cut down on overtime."
- "Let me tell you what I'm hearing. You would like to see the company set aside a certain amount of money for future growth and expansion, but you are concerned that the current amount we can afford won't add up to much in the short term."

It is important not to "parrot-phrase" someone's statements—that is, repeat back exactly the words that have been said. This will appear trite and naive. Paraphrasing takes practice and requires very careful, attentive listening.

Empathizing

Empathizing is the most powerful active listening skill. Like para-phrasing, it summarizes and reflects back to the speaker the content of what he or she has been saying. However, it goes one step further and demonstrates the listener's understanding of how the speaker is feeling. Understanding the concern, emotion, or motivational intent of what someone is saying is critical to understanding his or her inclinations.

Empathizing can be used very effectively to

- clarify feelings
- demonstrate a sense of concern
- increase the listener's credibility

- build additional trust
- heighten the speaker's enthusiasm and willingness to provide necessary information

It is important that the facilitator reflects the speaker's opinion or concern—not his or her own feelings or opinions.

One way to improve the focus on the group member is to minimize responses that begin with the word *I*; for example, "I understand your concern." This is sympathy, not empathy. A simple strategy for focusing on the speaker in a more empathic fashion is for the facilitator to start his or her summary or reflection with the word *you*; for example, "You're concerned about the future economic uncertainties and that hiring new people could be a problem if you need to downsize your department." In this example, the facilitator is reflecting concern from the speaker's point of view. Note that the empathic reflection does not suggest or imply that the facilitator agrees with the group member's perspective but simply reflects the facilitator's understanding of the speaker's concern.

Empathic responses contain an element of analysis. The feature that transforms them into active listening behavior is their tentative quality. When empathizing, the listeners cannot make pronouncements. Rather, they should choose their words carefully in order to indicate that they are simply sharing an interpretation and allowing the speaker to decide whether it is accurate.

Examples

- "You feel that you haven't been steered in the right direction by advisers in the past."
- "You are concerned about how the company will maintain profitability if anything happens to our overseas distribution channels."
- "You feel that your people won't be able to understand and use the new technology and that there may be some problems that could jeopardize our investment down the line."

The goal of empathizing is to give the person talking a clear indication of, "This is my understanding of what you are saying *and how you feel about it*."

Productive listening for a facilitator requires hard work. For managers, active listening takes on the further complexity of having to control or suppress tendencies to dictate or otherwise overly influence the responses of the group. While projecting neutrality, the manager is not relieved of listening critically and providing feedback that is both analytical and evaluative of the ideas being expressed. The responses that express disagreement may be appropriate as long as they appear to be unbiased or problem or solution oriented and as long as they are based on legitimate reasons.

NOTES

1. Edmund Carpenter and Marshall McLuhan, eds., *Explorations in Communication* (Boston: Beacon Press, 1960), 65.

2. Ibid., 66.

CHAPTER 8

Responding and Resolving

RESPONDING TO THE GROUP

Responding effectively is a skill that is used throughout the interaction with a group. It is especially important once the group's needs have been accurately assessed and together you begin to move toward recommendations and solutions that satisfy those needs.

KEY CONCEPTS

- Coordinating the ideas of the group and shaping them into a solution.
- Organizing the group output in such a way as to enable decision making.
- Stating your position on an issue based on your understanding of the facts and issues.
- Understanding how to handle objections, obstacles, and uncertainties.
- Questioning any objection before responding.
- Confirming acceptance of the resolution.

The Principle of Adaptation

Good communication requires both giving and receiving. Responding effectively means being clear and selecting words that narrow the range of possible interpretations of what you say. Generally, when framing a response, it is a good idea to apply what has been called the *principle of adaptation*, which says that people can communicate more clearly if they continually put themselves in the other person's shoes.

The principle of adaptation as applied to communication means fitting the words, phrases, and presentation style to the specific listeners. When facilitators find it necessary to present information, ideas, or the results of observations made about the group process, an attempt should be made to visualize the members of the group and to ask how this message might be received. Managers need to be particularly careful when presenting thoughts and ideas to a group composed primarily of subordinates. While the manager may feel that he or she is only making a suggestion, it is possible for all or some of the group members to receive the communication as a directive because of their relative power positions. When preparing to make a presentation to the group, a skilled facilitator will run through a mental checklist that includes questions like:

- How would you like to have this message presented if you were a member of the group?
- Would you be able to understand what is being said based on your prior experience with the subject matter?
- Are there aspects of what I am about to present that require additional definition or background in order to make my point clear?

It is useful to think of each opportunity to present as having two objectives: a primary objective and a secondary objective. The primary objective is to accomplish the specific goal or purpose of the message. Why are you saying these things? Are you explaining a procedure, coordinating ideas among group members, inserting new information into the discussion, summarizing the group product in order to put the discussion back on track? These factors need to be presented as orderly, clearly, and completely as possible.

The secondary objective focuses on the relationship aspects that exist between the facilitator and the members of the group. Beyond the content of the message being presented, the manner in which the message is delivered should support and enhance trust and credibility without being devoid of emotion. Most successful facilitators cultivate a style of presentation that is warm and sincere. It says to the members of the group, "I have your best interests at heart. And this is true even when we disagree."

We have already discussed the problem surrounding bypassing in Chapter 7. The same sensitivity that needs to be applied when listening effectively also needs to be applied to the presentation side of the equation. The words chosen must, to whatever extent possible, have the same meaning in the minds of both the presenter and the people receiving the message for successful communication to take place. Without carrying this discussion off to a tangent, suffice it to say that all organizations, including suborganizations in a single organization, tend to develop their own jargon, acronyms, and other verbal symbols that are peculiar to the particular group. Assuming that all the members of the group share the same communication vernacular, usage of these shorthand elements may communicate effectively and efficiently. However, when the group is not homogeneous, the facilitator needs to take care in selecting words that will not exclude some members of the group. He or she also needs to ask for definitions and clarifications about acronyms or jargon from the person in the group using them. The general rule for facilitators in response mode is to select words that are concrete rather than abstract, specific rather than general, positive rather than negative, and familiar rather than unfamiliar. Language that is concrete, specific, simple, and so on, decreases the chances of miscommunication.

Passive versus Active

In most presentation situations, such as giving a speech or making a formal presentation at a meeting, the use of the active voice is preferable. The active voice shows that someone or something is taking some action. The language is bolder and more direct and brings life to the presentation by making it interesting. For example, a presentation on a new process may include an evaluative sentence. Stated passively it might sound like this: "The new process being proposed is believed to be superior based on the investigation we have conducted." Stating the same point actively produces a much more powerful result: "Our investigations show that the new process is clearly superior."

However, the circumstances are different for the facilitator; there are many instances when use of the passive voice is precisely what is needed. A facilitator's use of the passive voice minimizes the potential for conflict. The passive voice is used

- when it is unknown who performed a particular action and you do not want to use the vague "someone" in the reference
- when you do not want to name a particular person because you are talking about a problem or an error and do not want to point an accusing finger
- when you want to deemphasize the role of a particular person because no one should be singled out for credit or blame

For example, if the group is having trouble making progress because of too much disagreement, the facilitator might use the active voice and say, "We're not getting anywhere because you people keep fighting too much." In this case the active voice challenges the group to defend itself and includes a judgment that puts the facilitator in a parental role. A better way to call the group's attention to the problem might be to say, "There seem to be some underlying issues causing conflict. Since our progress is being impeded, maybe we should focus for a time on those underlying issues and see if they can be resolved."

The principle of adaptation should be part of the basic mind-set of any facilitator. Successful responding requires the ability to see communication taking place from the group's point of view. People will not always respond in a predictable way. Responding effectively begins with realization that people do not automatically listen just because someone is talking. It cannot be assumed that other people care about the same things that the facilitator or other members of the group do. Much of the facilitator's work revolves around making sure the most complete and accurate communication is taking place.

When presenting or responding, the facilitator must carefully select and define his or her terms. Often it is necessary to periodically redefine or reexplain key terms that continue to arise in the discussion. A good way of helping to assure understanding is to ask members of the group to paraphrase or put into their own words their understanding of the words, concepts, or jargon used by others.

Organizing Your Responses

In addition to order, people also tend to look for completeness in the communication that they receive. When people perceive something that is incomplete, they fill in or add details on their own. If a whole response is not provided to the group, they may fill in missing details or examples and in doing so may turn the response into something un-intended.

In addition to the overall structure of the meeting, the facilitator can put some wholeness and structure into each response by talking about the links between the ideas being expressed. In this way, the group is not confused about what a particular response is relating to. Giving a sense of wholeness and structure to responses provides control over how ideas are perceived by others.

Here are some things to remember about providing structure and wholeness:

- Provide signposts and reminders for the group throughout the meeting to help it accurately interpret your responses.
- Written messages can be read and reread, but spoken responses come by only once.
- It is often helpful to repeat or restate what you say.
- You can often see what needs clarification or a structural connection by the looks on people's faces.
- Stay aware of any nonverbal feedback members of the group may be communicating so that you can recognize the need to go back over something.
- Remember that people can process only a limited amount of information at a time. If you let the group know why you are saying something, it is less likely to misinterpret what you are saying.
- Using examples and analogies in your responses makes them more interesting and less ambiguous.

RESOLVING ISSUES THAT AFFECT GROUP PROGRESS

Responding to Objections

You will often find it necessary to address some issue, previously hidden, that causes some members or the group as a whole to withhold commitment. Group members who fear making the wrong decision prefer to play it safe and do nothing.

Here are some possible group responses requiring resolution, followed by possible reasons to probe for:

- *I don't want to be here. I'm very busy and preoccupied with something else.* In this case, find out what the something else is about, actively listen, and use empathy to show willingness to understand the group member's issues.

- *I'm tough and I'm going to make it hard on you.* (This may be implied rather than stated.) Ask yourself why someone might want to do this. It could indicate personal immaturity and defensiveness, and you should react calmly and sensitively. The person may feel that his or her opinion is being undervalued.

- *I'm not convinced yet.* Ask more questions, because you have not yet found the real objection.

- *I need to be reassured so I can present this to someone else.* The group member is nervous about making the right decision. Give him or her confidence in the impending decision to accept the group's solution and advice about how to best present the decision to other interested parties.

- *I have a few questions I want answered.* Review your understanding of the progress so far and elicit any uncertainties the group member has.

- *I am a professional, and I am testing your competence, depth of knowledge, and persistence.* (Again, you will probably perceive this as an attitude rather than hear it as a statement.) If this appears to be the case, demonstrate your knowledge of the industry and/or experience dealing with similar issues and assert your desire to develop a helpful and ongoing business relationship.

Objections, Obstacles, and Uncertainties

Often the person who raises objections is showing a genuine interest in the work of the group. It is useful to think of objections in three ways:

1. An objection can be based on a misunderstanding or created by a potential solution that runs contrary to a group member's personal needs.
2. An obstacle is a special type of objection that is a barrier to commitment. It can be a money issue, a resource issue, or a general fear of change.
3. An uncertainty is a type of objection that is caused by lack of resolution among various options. Often a group is ready to commit to something, but more than one option sounds attractive. The group may be looking for you to make a strong case for one alternative.

Every objection must be treated with respect and diplomacy. There is no such thing as an unworthy objection. It is not the facilitator's role to attack or reject a person's objections. As a manager, when you aggressively attack an objection, you attack the individual's self-esteem.

Here are some things to remember about objections:

- Many facilitators dislike objections because they feel personally rejected.
- If you are presenting a solution, as in a persuasion meeting, group members may focus their attention on the problems they perceive with your recommendation and not the value of the proposal. This does not mean they don't think there is value in it. It often means they want time to think or want to feel in control of their decision.
- Objections can be a commitment signal. They indicate needs that haven't been addressed to the group's satisfaction. Objections can indicate an issue that simply did not come out in the earlier part of the discussion. They can indicate a need that was triggered by the very program or proposal you have presented. They can indicate a need that you have addressed but was not understood completely.

The Process for Handling Objections

When dealing with objections, obstacles, and uncertainties, the safest, most effective initial response is to move back in your skill set to questioning. Beginning with a question will clarify the specific nature of the objection or concern. Press for specifics to clarify as precisely as possible the person's concern:

- "Let me make sure I understand, Sally. Are you saying you'd prefer to put off the reorganization until a later date?"
- "When you say you're afraid you can't afford this, could you be more specific?"
- "John, when you say you don't believe you really need to outsource this function, do you mean you have other ways of meeting your financial goals?"

As you have already learned, when you have used a question you must next actively listen to demonstrate understanding of the person's point of view on the particular issue. Summarize the person's perspective without judging or evaluating it. This is done to show your understanding of the concern:

- "So you're concerned that the employment situation is uncertain for the future and that you may have difficulty meeting staffing requirements for this program."
- "What you're telling me is that the amount we're talking about setting aside may be more than the department can really afford in the budget at this time."

Having identified the real nature of the objection, the facilitator responds with appropriate information (specific features or technical data) that address the unique concerns of this particular group member. The more precise the response relative to the exact concern, the more likely the information offered will be satisfactory.

There are five alternative techniques you can use to respond. All five assume an understanding of why the person is uncertain. If this is not the case, then ask a question aimed at clarifying this before attempting one of the following.

1. Turn the objection, obstacle, or uncertainty into a question. This will give you time to think of an appropriate response to the problem.
2. If the issue has arisen because the person has misunderstood you, explain so that the misunderstanding is resolved.
3. If the issue has arisen because the person isn't very impressed with your proposal, go back to discussing the needs.
4. Agree that the person has a good point, then put the objection, obstacle, or uncertainty into a more favorable perspective and state more benefits to following your suggestion.
5. If an objection cannot be overcome at this meeting, admit it. It may be necessary to get an answer for the person from another party, or it may be necessary to redefine the approach and find an alternative solution. If you don't have the necessary information to offer an alternative solution, another meeting may be needed.

Once you have responded to an objection, you need to confirm the person's acceptance of your resolution of that objection by getting him or her to agree that the objection no longer exists:

- "Does that clarify the issue for you?"
- "Do you have a better understanding of how this works?"
- "Can I assume that you agree the amount we discussed is manageable and at the right level?"

- "Can you now see the benefits of this kind of approach over other alternatives we discussed?"

There are many pitfalls for managers who would be facilitators. Among the skill sets we have been discussing, the way a manager frames his or her responses to the group is perhaps the biggest failing. It is at the moment of framing a response that managers must put aside their notions of being in charge and present themselves in such a way that the group feels both safe and empowered to build a collective group product. No one will forget who is boss, even when the boss doesn't act like one.

CHAPTER 9

Closing and Getting Commitment

The most important and most often overlooked ingredient of the meeting is getting the commitment of the group to carry the action items forward. The successful facilitator never ends a meeting without achieving a commitment from the group, even if only to another meeting in the future. In concept, the entire facilitation process is a committing process.

KEY CONCEPTS

- Identify commitment signals.
- Employ the technique of assumed consent to bring your group to the commitment process.
- Gain commitment to action from the group.

Look for commitment from the opening moments of the meeting and obtain the group's approval to proceed. You are asking for commitment as you help the group identify problems and needs, move the group toward solutions to the identified problems, and obtain a commitment to action.

Commitment is taking place with the summary at the conclusion of each step in the facilitation process in order to communicate understanding, review the main points of discussion, and get agreement to proceed.

Once the group has moved to a decision or solution, the facilitator needs to ensure that it takes positive action. Commitment is a two-way street. On your part, you are committing yourself to the welfare of this group, to providing the best support to meet the group's needs, and to actively review the situation periodically for necessary adjustment. The group is committing to abide by the terms of the decision or solution and to take responsibility individually to see that the necessary actions are carried out.

COMMITMENT AND THE OBSTACLE OF AUTHORITY

When a manager facilitates, gaining commitment from a group of subordinates can be fairly simple. Often, however, that commitment does not run very deep, and the likelihood of the successful implementation of decisions and action plans is minimized. Various studies on the relationship of authority to decision making have revealed how easily people in positions of power can elicit compliant responses, even when they are unattended.[1]

When groups commit to courses of action based on their responses to authority, they can be led to foolish, inappropriate, or otherwise costly decisions. Effective facilitators, and in particular those who have real power, make efforts to mitigate the circumstances that could potentially lead to bad decisions. When groups are faced with a decision point in the presence of an authority figure, sometimes a kind of shared ignorance sets in. In this case, even though most, if not all, of the members of the group privately oppose the direction that the authority figure seems to be suggesting, they remain silent because of the perception that other group members are favorably disposed to the suggestion.[2] Another reason why false commitment occurs centers around the perception by less powerful group members that the manager has the right to determine the group's direction or that he or she possesses the resources with which to punish noncompliance.[3]

Managers who are sensitive to these issues have to apply good judgment in each case. After all, many attempts by managers to influence the decision-making process have positive rather than negative outcomes. If the manager suspects that the authority issue might be moving the group away from its goal, it is important to employ strategies that allow for and encourage challenges to the perceived authority-sponsored point of view.

One senior vice president with whom I had been working for some time as a coach was attempting to soften his autocratic style. He called a meeting of his direct reports and, as he tells it, calmly and without particular emphasis outlined his vision for the next year. He reports that he then asked the group to share with him their vision of what needed to be accomplished during the next year and was greeted with a chorus of "what you just said." Clearly the error here was laying out for the group his point of view. Based on their previous experience with this manager as an authority figure, there was little chance that any deviations from his stated plan would be verbalized.

No one would disagree that one hallmark of good management is providing clear and direct leadership through the presentation of goals and objectives that need to be accomplished. However, when the manager takes on the role of facilitator, the natural tendency to lead in this manner needs to be restrained to stimulate the level of participation required to gain consensus and a deeper group commitment to the decisions being made. In the case described above, given the existing perception of this manager, it would have been more productive to ask the group for their ideas and input before the manager stated his preferences. Also, because of his reputation as an authoritarian, his direct reports had little or no experience with empowerment. In fact, most of them had become quite comfortable simply bringing all of their problems to the manager. Over time by stepping back and insisting that his staff members bring him solutions along with problems they felt they could not solve on their own, this manager was able to free himself from a focus on task orientation and crisis management and move toward a more strategic role in the organization.

The Pressure for Uniformity

Many groups striving for solutions will divide into majority and minority positions on key issues. Pressure to conform to the majority opinion is frequently felt by the minority. Interestingly enough, this pressure for conformity seems to take place more in cohesive groups, those groups that have been working together for some time with a high level of effectiveness.[4]

Individuals who are members of cohesive groups want to maintain their ability to influence the group's actions. By disagreeing with the majority, a group member runs the risk of rejection and, once rejected, loses influence. This fear of rejection is a major factor in creating conformity. There are many circumstances where uniformity and conformity work very effectively for the group and the larger organization. These attributes are not intrinsically undesirable. It is when a majority position is in error or is otherwise indefensible that the pressure for uniformity constitutes a serious obstacle to those trying to keep the group headed toward its destination. The alternatives of either acquiescing or being rejected can leave group members with a sense of helplessness.

Another characteristic of excellent facilitation is the ability to sense and work against this pressure toward uniformity and to encourage and support constructive argument and the presentation of alternative opinions. Because the majority will naturally put pressure on the minority member or members to conform, the facilitator must act as a gatekeeper to keep the lines of communication open to minority positions and to manage or block majority aggressiveness that might place those with alternative opinions on the defensive.

Managing Status

The manager may not be the only person in the group who is perceived as having status. In fact, there are many times when a manager is called upon to facilitate a group that may contain people from other functional areas, or even his or her own, who occupy senior positions. Position in the organization is not the only determinant of status. Subcultures within organizations tend to develop opinion leaders who achieve high levels of status with other members without actually having prescribed rank. Facilitators, whether they are managers or not, need to control some of these tendencies in group process where they exist. The danger of not controlling the influence of high-status group members is that the group may be led in a direction that might not be taken, had the high-status people been neutralized. The greater influence that high-status group members have is usually attributed to others' perceptions that these individuals are more valuable to the group. This combines with a devaluation of their own opinions and judgments and a tendency to be uncritical of the ideas expressed by the more valued members. Research has shown that in a study of problem-solving groups, lower-status members having a correct solution were prone to endorse the one proposed by the highest-ranking member even when it was incorrect.[5]

This problem is not confined to problem-solving or decision-making groups. It is encountered frequently in information-gathering settings as well. For example, when conducting a focus group, I always provide an opportunity for the individual participants to anonymously express their feelings and opinions about the subject under consideration. This is accomplished by administering a questionnaire prior to the group experience and again polling them at the end of the process to see if quantitatively what they have to say agrees with the qualitative data collected from the focus group observations.

The key problem for the facilitator is to make a judgment as to whether the influence of high-status participants is interfering with the group's ability to achieve its goals. If members of the group have high status because they are in power positions in the organization, a certain amount of ingratiating behavior is inevitable The best strategy available to a facilitator in these circumstances is to select and employ an appropriate tool or technique that moves the process away from opinion toward a more objective assessment of the issues at hand. These tools and techniques will be discussed in greater detail in Part III.

COMMITMENT SIGNALS

Certain things the group may do or say will signal that it is ready to commit. When these signals appear, move to the commitment. Many experienced facilitators will tell you that it's just as easy to talk a group out of a commitment by talking past the point where it was ready to commit.

Commitment signals can be framed as questions or as positive statements relating to the solution on the table:

- nodding the head in a positive direction
- turning to look at each other in agreement
- sitting back and visibly relaxing
- picking up and studying a document

Here are some things to remember about responding to commitment signals:

- When these signals occur, begin to move toward commitment.
- Make the most of the group's positive attitude.

- If the facilitator has been successful at controlling all the other elements of the group process, the committing step should not be difficult.
- Think of commitment as gaining permission to move on to the next possible step.
- When a commitment is withheld, it is because the group believes there is nothing to gain from the actions under consideration.

Risk Issues

Risk is a key element of every decision. There is a broad range of psychological risk in all kinds of decision transactions. A risk issue is any personal feeling an individual may have that results in his or her believing he or she could lose something. Note the emphasis on personal. Risk issues are not concrete, quantifiable, objective realities waiting to be tinkered with and fixed up by the savvy facilitator. Risk issues arise from deep within the individual's experiences and value system.

Risk issues are obstacles that arise when the goals of the group are incompatible with the goals of the individual participants. This incompatibility can arise out of natural competitive tendencies between individuals or suborganizations or from underlying fears and concerns of a more personal nature. Risk issues that are not managed effectively have implications for both the task and social dimensions of performance. Productivity can be reduced and morale tends to be low. When individuals perceive their personal interests to be at odds with the goals of the group as a whole, it can be very difficult to prevent the emergence of a competitive climate. In another scenario, it is possible for group members to actually share the same risk issues, and these impediments will serve to inhibit commitment to what appears to be a logical course of action. Moving the group toward a cooperative approach to achieving its goals when the climate contains risk issues and competition is a test of the facilitator's skill. Direct appeals to become cooperative, to make commitments, and to place the interests of the group above those of the individual have little chance of working.

Risk issues cannot be overcome or talked around like an objection. A risk issue and an objection, although they may both impede the process, are two very different things. An objection is often the visible part of an underlying risk issue; or to put it in more scientific terms, the risk issue is the cause of the person's reluctance, while the objection is the effect. When someone raises an objection, it could be a signal that some underlying reason is causing trouble. That "something" is a risk issue. Another difference between an objection and a risk issue is that an objection is usually tangible and/or implementation related. A risk issue is not. Risk issues are related to the individual's mental picture, or concept, about the relationship; and like any mental picture, they're generally intangible and personal.

Overcoming an objection, therefore, is very different from dealing with a risk issue. It's no less than the difference between cause and effect, and facilitators who achieve success are never content simply to deal with effects. They know that dealing with causes is fundamental not only to getting commitment but also to forming any long-term business relationship.

Two related points bear some emphasis:

1. You cannot judge a risk issue. A risk issue is what someone is feeling, deep down, about what the group product will mean to him or her. There are ways to analyze and discuss and work with those feelings, but the one thing you should not do, ever, is to deny their validity. One of the surest ways to kill a relationship on the spot is to say to someone with a risk issue, "You shouldn't be feeling that way."

2. You cannot assume that you know what the particular risk issue is. Since the risk perception and noncommitment are always linked, it's safe to assume, when you cannot get commitment, that there's some risk issue involved. But it's hazardous to assume that you know what that risk issue is. It's easy for a facilitator to confuse one possible risk issue with another.

Before identifying a specific risk issue, the facilitator needs to be able to recognize the underlying fact that a risk issue exists. This is accomplished by watching for risk issue symptoms, outlined below:

• hesitation
• skepticism
• negative noises

Aggressiveness or passive resistance symptoms arrange themselves into a hierarchy. As the symptoms escalate, the probability of a commitment diminishes. If you're dealing with a merely hesitant person, you generally still have time to identify and resolve risk issues before the situation deteriorates. If the person has become outright hostile, it's more difficult to save the relationship, and it can affect the whole group.

To prevent this, you need to ask risk issue questions, which will show you where you are and what still needs to be done to move the process forward. Here are some examples.

- "Michael, I'm getting the impression that committing yourself to a particular vendor is making you uncomfortable. Can we talk about that?"
- "Donna, it's really important that you believe in what we're doing. Are you getting the sense that you are losing control of your ability to achieve your department's individual goals?"
- "I think you may need some additional explanation of the flexibility of this plan. You seem to feel you are being locked in. Is that right?"
- "Jim, you seem to be a little hesitant [or skeptical]. Is there something else we need to cover?"

Closing with a Risk Issue Question

Risk issue questions are a final test of a group's commitment. Every meeting should end with an understanding of what each group member should do to make his or her commitment level clear. Asking a risk issue question toward the end of a meeting is one good way of determining just what the current level of commitment is:

- "So, I'm feeling good about this plan, but you're the ones who have to live with it. How are you feeling right now?"
- "Are you all comfortable that we have covered all of the important issues?"

TECHNIQUES TO GAIN COMMITMENT

When you have received confirmation that the group has accepted a course of action or an explanation or resolution of an objection, it is time to ask for a commitment. To do this you should

1. confirm the group's needs as you understand them
2. summarize the specific benefits that the group has accepted during the course of the meeting and the ways in which those benefits satisfy the group's perceived needs

3. request the group's commitment to the plan

There are five basic types of commitment requests:

- assumed consent commitment
- direct commitment
- action commitment
- inducement commitment
- alternative commitment

Assumed Consent Commitment

Move directly into planning time frames for the group's deliverables, as though the group has already agreed to the actions:

- "All right, group, let's get out our calendars."

Direct Commitment

Ask questions that will give you a clue as to whether you need more discussion or can immediately ask for commitment:

- "Do you feel that we have covered everything we're looking for?"

Action Commitment

This is where you ask for a commitment by getting the group to take a positive step toward a future set of actions:

- "At this point, I think we should build a Gantt chart so that we can be sure to meet the completion requirements for this plan."

Inducement Commitment

Give the group an inducement to commit now, not later:

- "By making the decision now, we will avoid the possibility of higher prices that might be in effect by next year."

Alternative Commitment

Give the group a choice of several actions to take. In essence, it's not a choice of whether or not to commit but which action to commit to. One drawback for this type of choice is that the group may want to go back over all the details or take time to think it over.

- "Okay, group, I believe we have two excellent options to choose from. Which one of these solutions will work best for us?"

If additional objections or obstacles are raised, it should be natural for the facilitator to respond to these objections or differences. It is important for you to handle these differences or obstacles in a professional style, as you have earlier, or your behavior will appear inconsistent.

Here are some things to remember about committing:

- When you ask for a commitment, there are at least four possible responses:
    —a yes.
    —a qualified yes ("Yes, but . . .")
    —an objection/obstacle ("I'm still concerned about the . . .")
    —a flat no

In each of these four situations, an appropriate response on your part is critical.

1. If you receive a firm "Yes," the logical and appropriate next step is to complete the meeting. You may also want to reinforce the group's decision and the benefits that will derive from that decision.

2. If you receive a qualified "Yes, but," you need to clarify the group's reservations or concerns. Very often a group responding with a qualified yes is simply seeking some additional information, looking for some additional reassurance, or offering a relatively minor objection that may need clarification.

3. If you receive an objection, it is important to process this objection in the way that has helped you be successful to this point. Before attempting to answer an objection, it is important to question and actively listen to understand exactly what the concern is. Handled poorly, you may raise additional objections.

4. If you receive a flat "No," this should be a sign to you that you have not reached the commitment stage. It could also represent a defensive reaction on the part of the group who may feel that you're selling it a solution it hasn't bought into.

It is not safe for managers to assume that their role as a facilitator ends with the meeting. When consensus and commitment are achieved, they are never stronger than they are immediately following a particular meeting. However, they tend to erode over time. Without micromanaging, effective managers will periodically meet briefly with group members who have specific actions to carry out in order to provide guidance and support as needed. As a final action for any meeting where commitments have been received, it is often a good idea to schedule a follow-up meeting at some realistic interval so that the group as a whole can reflect, make adjustments, and if necessary, recommit to the tasks at hand.

NOTES

1. Stanley Milgram, *Obedience to Authority* (New York: Harper Colophon Books, 1969); Dennis S. Gouran, "The Watergate Cover-up: Its Dynamics and Its Implications," *Communication Monographs* 43 (1976): 176–186.

2. Robert L. Schanck, "A Study of a Community and Its Groups and Institutions Conceived of as Behaviors of Individuals," *Psychological Monographs* 43 (1932): 195.

3. George C. Homans, *Social Behavior: Its Elementary Forms*, 2nd ed. (New York: Harcourt, Brace, Jovanovich, 1974), 193–224.

4. Stanley Schacter, "Deviation, Rejection and Communication," *Journal of Abnormal and Social Psychology* 46 (1951): 190–207.

5. E. Paul Torrance, "Some Consequences of Power Differences on Decision Making in Permanent and Temporary Three-Man Groups," *Research Studies Washington State College* 22 (1954): 130–140; Muzafer Sherif, B. Jack White, and O.J. Harvey, "Status in Experimentally Produced Groups," *American Journal of Sociology* 60 (1955): 370–379.

PART III

Facilitation Tools

In their quest for more effective and efficient meetings with more positive outcomes, managers have at their disposal a number of proven processes to support these efforts. These processes, often called facilitation tools, provide a framework and a roadmap for moving discussions forward, enhancing objectivity, and helping in the decision-making process. The tools discussed in Part III are grouped according to where they might apply in a facilitation timeline. For example, there are tools that can be associated with planning a meeting that are used before the meeting begins. Others are useful in conducting meetings and may fall into subcategories, depending on the type of output that is required of the group. Still others may be useful for evaluating meetings or keeping track of follow-up tasks. Some tools have broad application and are useful in several different types of meetings. Therefore, as we discuss a tool, we will also look at various scenarios for its application.

The tools included in Part III are not meant to be comprehensive. Several excellent resources can be used to expand the number of tools at the manager's disposal. The tools included here have been chosen as the most likely tools to be used by managers as facilitators.

CHAPTER 10

Planning

In our busy lives it is easy to overlook some very important things. One of these things is setting aside some time for planning. The research available along with anecdotal information attests to the fact that managers are spending a major proportion of their time in meetings. Presumably, they are facilitating a large portion of these meetings.

KEY CONCEPTS

- Taking time for planning.
- Participant and group issues.
- Premeeting tasks.
- Stating the objectives to be accomplished.
- Selecting and communicating with the participants.
- Choosing a strategy.
- Selecting tools.
- Scheduling time and location.
- Organizing the agenda.
- Arranging the physical environment.

PLANNING TIME IS HARD TO FIND

As discussed in Chapter 2, managers are spending considerable time in meetings of various types and under various conditions. While the time spent in meetings has increased somewhat in recent years, the fast pace of today's business environment has given rise to more impromptu meetings. Such meetings are difficult to prepare for. Fortunately, many impromptu meetings are held in order to address an immediate problem, often of a technical nature, and the focus of the meeting is on matters already familiar to the participants.

Many managers, however, procrastinate on planning for their meetings even when there is sufficient advance time to set them up. By not planning carefully, these managers are missing an opportunity to build efficiency into the schedules of their staff and themselves and create a perception of competent leadership. Nothing turns a staff against the manager more quickly than the feeling that they are wasting their time.

Substantial gains in time and productivity could be realized by managers using procedures designed to reduce the number and especially the duration of meetings. Those managers who achieve higher levels of efficiency and productivity do so through a concerted effort in planning.

SETTING OBJECTIVES FOR MEETINGS

Planning begins with the setting of objectives. The facilitator of a meeting must determine the exact objectives to be accomplished. Objectives must be

- determined before participants are selected or invited
- stated in a way that is consistent with the type of meeting planned and the kind of participation expected
- stated in a language that is clear, specific, and measurable (indicate performance criteria: how much, by what date)
- oriented to participants, not the leader
- stated as results to be accomplished (who, what, how much, when, and where)
- discussed with participants before the meeting
- stated in an agenda

Examples of Objectives

If an information-giving meeting is planned, objectives may be stated in the following manner:

1. Participants will explain the five steps in the new review policy.

2. Participants will evaluate the present status of the investigation.

3. Participants will examine the change in procedures including:

 a. Reasons for the change

 b. The new procedures

NOT

1. The leader will describe the new review policy.

2. The leader will give a status report of the project.

3. The leader will explain the change in procedures.

If the purpose of the meeting is to solve a problem, the objectives could be stated as follows:

1. How can the budget be reduced by 15 percent for fiscal year 2003?

2. How can the installation process be overhauled to accommodate the 20 percent increase in clients expected by January 2004?

3. How can staff turnover be reduced by 25 percent by October 31?

NOT

1. Budget reduction for this year.

2. Improved installation process.

3. Staff turnover.

If a fact-finding meeting is planned to brainstorm a subject and gather facts, objectives could be:

1. What are the possible ways of reducing staff turnover by 25 percent?

2. What are the possible ways to reduce travel costs by 10 percent during the next quarter?

3. What are the possible ways of improving the client training process?

NOT

1. Staff turnover.

2. Travel costs.

3. Client training.

By stating objectives as action items, the facilitator shapes his or her thinking toward a desired outcome and makes the charge to the group more specific. It also begins to point the way toward tools that will help in the meeting process.

THE AGENDA

Some leaders confuse *agenda* with *objectives*. Objectives are *things to be accomplished*. The agenda is the *order* in which subjects will be covered; the sequence in which objectives will be accomplished. Agendas should indicate

- time allocated for each agenda item
- who should do what for each agenda item
- who should be present for each agenda item

Structuring the Agenda

The agenda's structure determines the flow of the meeting and should correspond with the stages of the meeting. Meetings have the following stages:

1. *Opening stage*: Get the attention of the participants.
2. *Imparting information stage*: State the purpose of the meeting and clarify meeting objectives.
3. *Group acceptance stage*: State the time limits and ask for participants' response to the sequence of objectives on the agenda.
4. *Stimulating discussion stage*: Focus on specific agenda topics and direct the discussion to accomplish the objectives and get participant satisfaction.
5. *Conclusion stage*: Restate the objectives, summarize the information and decisions, and state plans for future actions or meetings.

Example of a Problem-Solving Meeting Agenda

1. Introduction (a 5-minute talk to get attention)
   a. A story related to the subject
   b. Explanation of why the group is there
   c. Explanation of how the group can help solve the problem

   d. Dramatic examples of the problem

   e. Clear statement of the problem

2. Solving the problem (a 45-minute structured discussion)

   a. Causes (15 minutes)

     • What caused the problem?

     • Why do we have the problem?

   b. Criteria (5 minutes)

     • What changes should a good solution to the problem cause?

   c. Suggested solutions (15 minutes)

     • What can be done to improve the situation?

     • What suggestions do you have for solving the problem?

   d. Best solutions (10 minutes)

     • Of the ideas suggested, which ones meet the criteria?

     • Which of these suggestions aren't practical?

     • What is the best solution to our problem?

3. Summary and conclusions (10 minutes)

   a. Restatement of the problem

   b. What has been decided

   c. What will be done about it

THE FACILITATION PLANNING KIT

This tool can be used to walk through the key planning stages. It is presented here filled out with example responses indicated in italics (see Figure 10.1). A blank copy of the Facilitation Planning Kit can be found as Appendix B.

What: The Facilitation Planning Kit is a step-by-step process for the facilitator to follow to ensure that he or she is properly prepared for the meeting.

When: The Facilitation Planning Kit is used as soon as practical prior to the scheduled meeting. The kit is also useful for developing some parameters prior to the scheduling of a meeting or several meetings.

How: Answer the questions as they are posed in sequence as you move through the kit. In some cases, you may have to skip over a part and return to it later when the information is available or issues have been clarified.

Timing: Time for filling out a kit will vary according to the complexity of the meeting. However, care should be taken when preparing the objectives and the agenda, and this should take approximately one hour.

Figure 10.1
Facilitation Planning Kit—Example

Today's Date: *mm/dd/yy*

Meeting Date: *mm/dd/yy*

Meeting Purpose:

What is the purpose for calling the meeting?

> *The group has been called together to share information about a new change, to figure out why people are resisting change, and to agree on a method to collect customer satisfaction.*

Is a meeting the best format to achieve your purpose? (Yes/No) If answering no, what is a better strategy?

> *Meeting is the best strategy.*

Meeting Type

What kind of meeting are you preparing?

	Information giving
✓	*Fact finding*
✓	*Problem solving*
	Persuading
	Training
✓	*Decision making*

Participant List

Who are the participants and what value does each bring to the subject matter?

What is each participant expected to contribute to the meeting? Each person should know why he or she has been selected to attend; e.g., particular information or expertise.

Participant	Title/function	Value
John A.	*Supervisor*	*Line input*
Jane C.	*Office Manager*	*Staff input*
Mark F.	*Sales Manager, East*	*Field input*
Sally K.	*Sales Manager, West*	*Field input*
Bob S.	*Communications Manager*	*Companywide perspective*
Mary V.	*Budget Planning Manager*	*Financial data*
Jack W.	*Manager/Facilitator*	*Facilitator*

Figure 10.1 (continued)

Meeting Objectives

What are the *critical success factors/desired outcomes*? By the end of the meeting, what do you and the group want to have achieved?

Examples:
- *Created a detailed work plan for implementing the new purchasing procedure.*
- *Determined the three top priority issues for improving customer service.*
- *Everyone understands the scope of the production problem facing the company.*

Are there additional *learning objectives*? If so, what are they? Are there things you want the participants to learn that would help them function better together?

Examples:
- *The group learns to discuss emotional issues calmly.*
- *Fred develops confidence to contribute to group discussions.*
- *The group sees how complex the project is.*

Participant and Group Issues

What assumptions can you make about this group and this particular meeting? What are some individual or group issues/problems for which you should prepare?

It is important to anticipate the group's behavior before designing an agenda.

Examples:
- *The group will have a wide range of opinions and feelings about these issues.*
- *The group is experienced and works well together, so we should be able to get a lot accomplished.*
- *They will be quiet at first because they are all front-line staff and new to the organization.*
- *There may be left-over hostility between Joe and Barbara because of the heated discussion at the end of the last meeting.*

What are your contingency plans if problems develop?

You try to design an agenda that will lead to a smooth meeting. However, problems sometimes occur.

Examples:
- *Cut the meeting short if emotions run too high.*
- *Speak to Tom during the break if he continues to cut people off.*
- *If, because of the group size, we have difficulty moving forward, break the group into small task teams and delegate pieces of the problem.*

Meeting Length

What is your initial estimate about how much time is required for the meeting?

The meeting will run two hours with a 20-minute break in the middle.

Figure 10.1 (continued)

Premeeting Tasks

Facility arrangements

Location:	*Boardroom*
Room size:	*Medium*
Cost estimates:	*NA*
Seating/table arrangement:	*Large conference table—chairs around all four sides.*

Equipment arrangements

✓	*Overhead projector/screen*
	LCD
	VCR/monitor
✓	*Flip charts*
✓	*White board*
✓	*Conference calling*

Additional arrangements

✓	*Memo to participants*
✓	*Organize information*
✓	*Distribute information prior to meeting*
✓	*Confirm attendance*

THE MEETING

Meeting Strategy

Review the meeting's purpose and objectives, your assumptions, the group's makeup, and issues. What would be a general strategy for achieving the objectives?

Examples*:*
- *If this is the kickoff meeting for an ongoing project, you would want to allow sufficient time for people to understand the purpose of the group and learn about the others' knowledge and expertise.*
- *If a lot has to be accomplished in a short amount of time, your initial remarks would address this issue and motivate them to pull together to accomplish the objectives.*

Meeting Activities

List the activities needed for each phase of the meeting. Estimate how long each activity will take. This section allows the facilitator some freedom to brainstorm ideas before developing a specific agenda.

Phase I: Opening
  Examples:
- *Orient the group and tell them what their role is. (5 min.)*

Figure 10.1 (continued)

- *Have the EVP outline the problem. (10 min.)*
- *Have individual members discuss their experience with the problem. (15 min.)*

Phase II: Middle
    Examples:
- *Complete a cause and effect diagram. (30 min.)*
- *Come to consensus about the critical problem areas. (15 min.)*
- *Decide how to get more information about each of the problem areas. (20 min.)*

Phase III: Ending
    Examples:
- *Review any assignments.*
- *Agree on next meeting date.*

Tools and Techniques

Which tools and techniques will support the meeting activities?

Choose from the array of tools and techniques that can help you conduct the meeting efficiently and effectively.

    Example:
    Force Field Analysis may be the right tool to use, but you are concerned that the younger, newer people in the group will have difficulty adding their thoughts. You may want to use the technique of having everyone write down two to three ideas on a piece of paper before starting the discussion.

The Agenda

Using the following format, write a final version of the desired outcomes and develop a detailed agenda.

Desired Outcomes:

The team will be informed as to where we currently are in the project.

Agenda Format:

Time	Activity	Person	Desired Outcome
2:00	*Introduction.*	*Jack W.*	*Orientation, agenda, hand-off to Jane C.*
2:10	*Presentation of data from office staff.*	*Jane C.*	*Evaluate hypotheses regarding office staff.*
2:45	*Presentation of data from sales staff.*	*Mark F. Sally K.*	*Evaluate hypotheses regarding sales staff.*
3:30	*Summarize and adjourn.*	*Jack W.*	*Clarify, confirm, develop new action points if necessary.*

Figure 10.1 (continued)

Roles and Responsibilities

What are participant natural roles, or which assignments need to be made?

- Group Leader: *NA*
- Facilitator: *Jack W.*
- Recorder: *Bob S.*
- Presenters: *Jane C., Mark F., Sally K.*
- Timekeeper: *Jack W.*
- Follow-up: *Jack W.*

Meeting Ground Rules

If the group has not established meeting ground rules, be prepared to discuss this and help them generate a list. Be prepared with a list of your own in order to start the discussion.

Examples:
- *Don't talk while others are speaking.*
- *Start and end meetings on time.*
- *Everyone is responsible for achieving our objectives.*
- *Come to meetings prepared.*
- *Group can add or modify ground rules over time if new needs are identified.*

Supplementary Tools for Planning

It may be useful to employ some tools that help develop or expand sections of the Planning Kit. Here are a few that managers may find helpful in keeping them focused and covering all the bases.

Tool Selection Checklist

Data Collection
- What data exist?
- Do we need more data?
- How should the data be collected?

Data Analysis
- How are the data organized?
- What type of analysis should be applied to the data?
- Do the data need to be grouped or organized in a specific manner?
- Is there a tool that can help facilitate analysis of these data?
- Can the outcomes of analysis be mapped visually?

Presentation
- Are the data and subsequent analysis easy to understand?
- Are the relationships between various components clearly discernible?
- How can we put our analysis into action?

Consideration of these questions will lead the facilitator toward selecting tools and processes that help ensure understanding among all group members and produce results.

Scheduling realities may not allow for the level of comprehensive planning represented by the Facilitation Planning Kit. However, whether or not completely filled out, the categories provide a blueprint for setting and managing the facilitator's expectations for the meeting.

Many managers find checklists tedious or somehow beneath them. Yet if a manager wants to improve both the perception and the reality of his or her leadership, it begins with planning.

CHAPTER 11

Conducting

With so many excellent tools available, it is amazing how infrequently they are used to aid in the collection and organization of data. Tools for conducting group sessions fall into four broad categories:

1. tools for generating information
2. tools for organizing information
3. tools for analyzing information
4. tools for driving commitment

Tools stimulate interaction and focus members' attention on the task at hand. They are an excellent means of supporting the agenda and moving the process efficiently forward.

KEY CONCEPTS

- Identify the groups you presently belong to and those you are likely to join in the future.
- Match tools to the personal and group goals to be accomplished.
- Choose the most effective decision-making method for a group task.
- Adapt your leadership style to meet the group's needs and objectives.

BRAINSTORMING

What passes for brainstorming in most corporate settings is not really brainstorming—it is list generating (Figure 11.1). Brainstorming is a

Figure 11.1
List

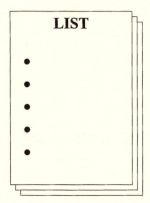

very specific technique originally developed for use in "think tank" environments. For brainstorming to take place, there are two important rules to follow.

1. All of the participants must be willing to say whatever comes to mind without editing.
2. The entire group must suspend any form of judgment on what is being said.

The idea behind brainstorming is that synapses are stimulated by the variety of input available in the environment, and ideas are generated that ordinarily wouldn't be thought of if someone else hadn't said something that triggered the thought. So even though a suggestion by one member might be outlandish and unworkable, this utterance may cause another member to create a modification that makes the idea plausible. The output is captured on a list and then, and only then, criteria are developed to evaluate the various options. This is difficult in settings that do not have the level of trust and the experience of working together as a group for long periods of time. Any suggestion of judgment or criticism by any one member will destroy a brainstorming session.

AFFINITY DIAGRAM

The affinity diagram (Figure 11.2) is also referred to as the K-J diagram after Japanese anthropologist Jiro Kawakita (denoted K-J by

Figure 11.2
Affinity Diagram

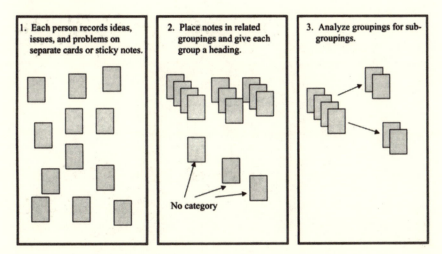

1. Each person records ideas, issues, and problems on separate cards or sticky notes.

2. Place notes in related groupings and give each group a heading.

No category

3. Analyze groupings for sub-groupings.

the Japanese custom of last name first) developed an inductive approach to synthesizing large amounts of data into manageable chunks based on themes that emerged from the data themselves.[1]

The K-J method uses a team approach to develop affinity diagrams in which each element of data is grouped with other similar elements of data. The K-J technique requires an open mind from each participant, encourages creativity, and like brainstorming, avoids criticism of "strange" ideas.

Typically, each data element is recorded onto a card or Post-it note. The cards are well shuffled to eliminate any preexisting order and are then grouped based on feelings rather than logic. The impression or image given by each statement suggests the group to which that card has the greatest affinity rather than any preconceived category. When a few cards are grouped, they are labeled with a description that captures the essence of their meaning. Card groups are then assembled into a larger diagram with relationships between the groups of cards indicated. The end result is a diagram showing the top 5 to 10 relationships among the data.

FISHBONE/CAUSE AND EFFECT DIAGRAM

Fishbone or cause and effect diagrams are so named because of their appearance (Figure 11.3). The concept is attributed to Kaoru Ishikawa

Figure 11.3
Fishbone Diagram

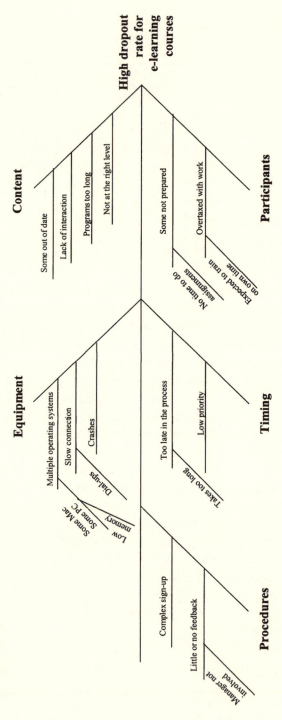

of Tokyo University around 1943. Ishikawa was working on ways to help managers increase the quality of their products. He was one of the first to develop the notion of companywide quality control. He promoted the notion of continued customer service and saw quality improvement as a continuous process. As a support for his approach, Ishikawa developed his cause and effect diagram by using a fishbone diagram. A facilitator can accumulate and display all of the possible causes of a result and hopefully find the issues that need addressing.[2]

Managers can use fishbone diagrams as part of the facilitation process to systematically list the different causes that can be attributed to a problem. These diagrams are particularly useful for identifying the reasons why a process goes out of control.

A cause and effect diagram creates an organized pictorial display of factors contributing to a problem. The "spine" is represented by a line pointing to a problem. The branches off the spine represent the main categories of potential causes (or solutions).

Managers can use this type of diagram as an effective tool for studying processes for planning. The visual arrangement often leads to greater understanding of a problem and facilitates the development of a larger list of contributing factors. The cause and effect diagram should not be used for brainstorming. It comes into play when the problem is well understood by the group and the contributing factors are known individually and collectively by the group. As such, it is a diagnostic rather than an analytic tool.

Using the Tool

Since the fishbone diagram is designed to highlight the cause and effect relationship, the facilitator can use a systematic approach to help assure that all the available data are collected from the group. To stimulate discussion about causes, the facilitator can use various versions of the four following questions:

1. What are the factors contributing to the problem? Such as concrete objects like machines and materials.
2. Why are these conditions causing the problem? Such as motivation or lack of training.
3. When are the problems occurring? Such as in a sequential process.

4. Where are the problems occurring? Such as a specific location, production line, or shipping department.

Additional questions can be used to focus the group's attention on issues directly associated with the type of business. For example, if the manager is examining manufacturing problems, questions can be posed to the group concerning manpower, materials, methods, machines, and measurements (the five Ms). For problems associated with service industry issues, the questions may relate to employees, supplies, procedures, environment, and customers.

There are generally three steps to creating the diagram:

1. Define and delimit the effect being analyzed. Write the problem on the right side of a flip chart with a large arrow (the spine) pointing to it.
2. Based on the discussion, identify and represent the main categories of potential causes as "ribs" attached to the spine. These may be standard categories like People, Materials, Machines, and Methods.
3. Discuss each major category and identify secondary and tertiary causes. Attach each specific cause to an appropriate main cause.

Often a subcause could be listed logically under more than one main cause.

Figure 11.3 depicts the output of a hypothetical discussion regarding low attendance for e-learning programs. The diagram might be significantly more complex if an actual discussion had taken place. However, the example points to the key factors associated with the fishbone process. Looking at the diagram, we can assume that five main categories of cause were associated with the high dropout rate. Group members felt the content needed work, that there was resistance among the participants based on job-related commitments, and that the equipment that the learners were supposed to use lacked standardization and sufficient power to handle the programs effectively. In addition, complex procedures and the way the programs are scheduled in the learning process also have associated hindrances.

Having employed this tool, the manager is now in a position to systematically analyze for causal components of the problem and to begin to formulate solutions. At this stage any number of actions could be proposed. For instance, subgroups of the main group could be assigned to each of the major categories as a work group to come back with a fuller analysis and some suggestions for managing the difficulties. In another approach, the entire group could evaluate each of the cause factors and assess their ability to have an impact. For example, the organization may be unwilling to make the necessary financial commitment to upgrade and standardize all the equipment. Therefore, this is a factor out of the immediate control of the group. However, the interplay between problems with content and problems with technology might be assigned a high priority since adjustments in the way content is constructed and delivered would have an impact on some of the technology problems.

The fishbone diagram is a very attractive and effective tool. It is easy to learn and apply. To derive the maximum benefit from this tool, managers need to carefully define the problems or effects they want to analyze. In the previous example, if the manager had failed to limit the problem to the e-learning dropout rate and instead began a discussion about what's wrong with e-learning, the group would have been unavoidably drawn into tangents that would not be productive for the diagnosis of the problem. When using a tool such as this, the manager's skill and understanding of facilitation principles are put to the test. The successful facilitator must be open to different ideas and must manage the process so that political issues and dominant team members do not contaminate the output with their personal agendas.

FORCE FIELD ANALYSIS

Force field analysis is another exceptional tool that provides managers with the opportunity to effect change. The technique, and the resulting tool, was developed by Kurt Lewin. Lewin's force field theory asserts that in any situation there are forces that struggle for equilibrium. This equilibrium is achieved through a balance of both driving and restraining forces. Driving forces are those forces affecting a situation that push the situation in a particular direction. They can be viewed as forces that promote change such as productivity or quality improvements, monetary and other incentives, and competitive forces. Restraining forces are acting to offset the pressure from the driving forces. Such things as lack of financial resources, apathy, and lack of or poor equipment might fall into this category. If the forces offset one another completely, we have equilibrium and status quo. Lewin suggests that change cannot occur by increasing the driving forces alone, since by doing so it immediately gives rise to restraining forces to offset the new driving forces. He sees the key to arriving at meaningful change as the removal or diminishing of the restraining forces.[3]

This approach to problem solving and action planning can be adapted to many situations. It is useful as part of a visioning exercise because it forces the group to examine the status quo in contrast to where they want to be. Long-range strategic planning can be addressed by considering goals for two-year, five-year, or longer periods. In any case the forces can be identified and plans developed to increase driving forces and decrease restraining forces over whatever time span is appropriate.

This tool aids teams in identifying factors that are either enabling or hindering the team from moving forward in certain areas. By identifying the driving and restraining forces, solutions can be developed that will shift the forces and allow for positive actionable solutions.

This technique is used when teams get bogged down or feel immobilized and desire to develop positive, actionable solutions. It is also used as a change model that provides teams with a technique for analysis of the current situation. Understanding the current situation enables teams to develop positive change strategies.

Using the Tool

Define the problem and set the goals of the session. Divide a flip chart, white board, or other medium in half by drawing a vertical line down the middle of the page. Driving forces will be listed on the left side of the line, restraining forces on the right. Forces are represented by arrows pointing to the middle line.

The group is then asked to develop a list of all the factors that are forces for change. These are listed in one column with arrows pointing toward the center line. Next, or concurrently, they are asked to list all of the factors that resist change, and these are listed in a similar manner in the opposite column. Since the factors listed will have qualities of relative significance and impact, it is useful for the group to make additional judgments about each factor. For example, a numerical rating system might be developed to reflect the group's view of the relative strength of each factor. Also, depending on the issue, the group may want to examine how much impact they as a group can have to either enhance or diminish a particular factor. Along these lines, if one of the major restrainers is a serious dip in the economy, there is relatively

Figure 11.4
Force Field Analysis

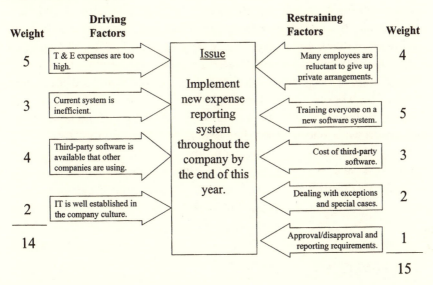

Weight	Driving Factors	Issue	Restraining Factors	Weight
5	T & E expenses are too high.	Implement new expense reporting system throughout the company by the end of this year.	Many employees are reluctant to give up private arrangements.	4
3	Current system is inefficient.		Training everyone on a new software system.	5
4	Third-party software is available that other companies are using.		Cost of third-party software.	3
2	IT is well established in the company culture.		Dealing with exceptions and special cases.	2
14			Approval/disapproval and reporting requirements.	1
				15

little the group can do about it. On the other hand, if a restraining factor is ineffective deployment of staff, the group can potentially have significant impact. Figure 11.4 provides a hypothetical example of a force field analysis.

In this example a manager may be chairing a task force examining the implementation of a new expense reporting system. The diagram presents a few factors of what may be a much more complex issue. However, as an illustration, it shows how a force field diagram can be used. An examination of this diagram provides the group with additional points for analysis and discussion as well as leading them toward action planning. Here are some possible discussion outcomes to reduce the restraining factors:

• Additional research can be done to pinpoint why employees are reluctant to follow current policies. For example, if the company has a preferred travel agency and nearly half the employees don't use it, find out why not and what changes or incentives can be put in place to gain more compliance. An effective action on this point could reduce the level of restraints significantly.

• Opening up discussion with the third-party software vendor on the training issue could yield models for training or shifts in responsibility that would place less of a burden on your organization.

• The costs may be negotiable or prorated over a long period of time.

Any significant impact on those three restraining factors could alter the balance that currently presents as being against the plan to a more favorable outcome for change. Force field analysis is a useful technique for providing a broad-based understanding of the pros and cons of a particular plan or strategy. It points the group toward the areas that need to be worked on to make a plan effective. It should be apparent that these diagrams and the principles behind them are often best used in concert with one another. For example, the restraining factor concerning employees being reluctant to give up their own private arrangements is a cause and effect situation. Either during this discussion or a subsequent discussion the facilitator might call upon a fishbone cause and effect diagram to break that problem down into its component parts.

MULTI-VOTING

Multi-voting is a very useful technique that can be used in various forms with both small and large groups. This tool is used to establish priorities, to evaluate a list of ideas, or to highlight specific areas of consensus and polarization within a group. The multi-voting process supports active group involvement because each group member participates equally. Using multi-voting on its own does not ensure that good decisions will result. Also, it is probably not the best option when a unanimous decision is what is being sought. However, it can be valuable in limiting the options when there is difficulty in reaching a consensus.

Using the Tool

While there are many variations, the basic multi-voting technique calls for displaying the items under consideration on a flip chart or other medium. If the objective is to prioritize or whittle down a large list to fewer items, each group member may be limited as to the number of items they may vote on. For example, each group member may be able to vote for half the number of items on the list or some other limitation agreed to in advance. In other configurations, each group member is provided with only one vote or is allowed to vote several

Figure 11.5
Multi-Voting Example 1: Client Profile

CLIENT PROFILE

1. Select six attitudes or behaviors you feel are typical of most of the people who call the customer service center.

2. Prioritize your list from 1-6, with 6 being the most prevalent and 1 the least prevalent.

_____ Accepting	_____ Skeptical
_____ Friendly	_____ Indifferent
_____ Hostile	_____ Grateful
_____ Confused	_____ Defensive
_____ Aggressive	_____ Frightened
_____ Stressed	_____ Passive
_____ Impatient	_____ Abusive
_____ Understanding	_____ Cooperative
_____ Avoiding	_____ Evasive
_____ Suspicious	_____ Aloof
_____ Accommodating	_____ Eager
_____ Diplomatic	_____ Unenthusiastic
_____ _____	_____ _____
_____ _____	_____ _____
_____ _____	_____ _____

times for the same item, thereby indicating the strength of his or her belief in that item.

A common and effective way of conducting the vote is to provide each of the group members with adhesive dots. If the group is small, there may be some advantage to providing each person with different colored dots so that the voter can be identified and be asked to provide a rationale for their selections. Alternatives to adhesive dots are a simple show of hands or the use of ballots. However, the visual impact provided by the dots tends to be more compelling.

I have used multi-voting in several situations with good success. Two examples are provided below. The multi-voting exercise represented in Figure 11.5 has been used effectively to identify characteristics, needs, and expectations of typical clients. Staff working in client-facing situ-

Figure 11.6
Multi-Voting Example 2: Sales Development Initiatives

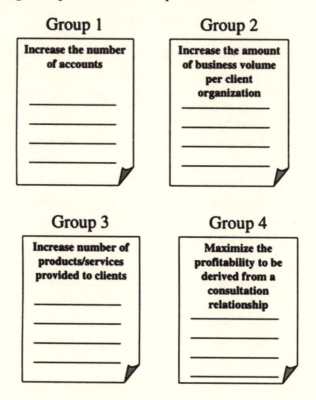

ations such as call centers and technical support operations tend to remember those interactions that are the most extreme rather than the more typical interactions that occur. This multi-voting exercise helps the group to see commonalities among the larger portion of their client group. It also underscores the fact that all of the people in the environment are experiencing basically the same things. Based on the output from this exercise, it is then possible to develop some understanding and resulting behaviors that are more effective for addressing the customer's needs, establishing a better climate, and making the client interactions easier to manage.

Another use of multi-voting is for the generation of new ideas. The exercise represented by Figure 11.6 has been used effectively with large sales teams to reexamine current approaches and develop new and creative initiatives for achieving greater sales volume. The larger group is divided into four teams. Each team is assigned one of the four initiatives. The individual teams generate lists of ideas that they post on flip charts. Each team is provided with adhesive dots for multi-voting. Each group then shifts one position to another group's work space. The vacating group leaves one spokesperson to explain or otherwise amplify on the ideas presented on their chart. The visiting team then votes for those ideas that they feel have the most potential. The groups then shift to another position, and the process is repeated until all of the groups have had an opportunity to vote on the output that each of them has produced. A list is then compiled of the ideas and initiatives that have received the most votes. The next step in the process calls for more concrete analysis and development of each of these suggested ideas, resulting in action planning and the assigning of responsibility. Ideas that were not selected for consideration at this meeting because of their low vote total are not discarded; they are placed in a "parking lot" (a separate list) that will not be further discussed at this session but will be reconsidered at subsequent meetings down the line.

There are many additional variations of multi-voting, and a skilled facilitator will look for opportunities to employ this tool to energize the group and encourage creativity.

PARETO ANALYSIS

The Pareto analysis is so named because of the observations of Vilfredo Pareto in the late 1800s. The observation attributed to his penchant for gardening was that 80 percent of the land in Italy was owned by 20 percent of the population.[4] He further observed that 80 percent of productive plants in his garden were derived from 20 percent of the seed. The Pareto analysis has proven to be a very useful and durable tool. Applying the Pareto principle, or "80-20 rule," as it is sometimes called, to group process suggests that among any group of items or factors influencing the outcome, relatively few will account for most of the effect. Facilitators can use Pareto analysis during the course of a discussion by developing charts and tables that illustrate the 80-20 rule. For example, if a cause and effect analysis is undertaken resulting in a fishbone diagram presenting a relatively long list of potential causes, the facilitator might suggest the application of a Pareto analysis as the next step. Discussion about the relative contribution of the various causes on the list leads the group toward identification of the "vital few." In the case of problem solving, the vital few are those 20 percent of the total causes that contribute 80 percent of the problem. The 80 percent and 20 percent differentiation is not sacrosanct. In some cases, 10 percent of the causes will create 90 percent of the problem. The benefit of using Pareto is that it helps the manager identify where he or she can get the largest returns by deploying resources.

Using the Tool

The power of a Pareto analysis lies in the application of the principle rather than a strict adherence to a particular form. Tool platforms, such as spreadsheets, charts, and graphs, can all be used to capture and analyze the results of a Pareto analysis. In the following example (see Figure 11.7), the technology area of a large software firm servicing the financial services industry needed to cut costs because of a downturn in the economy. This company had prided itself for a number of years on providing the same high level of service to all of its clients. A cost analysis of the services being provided yielded information suggesting that large portions of the client base were not producing sufficient revenue to cover the costs of the services provided. A spreadsheet was produced comparing the revenue of every client for three years. Since the number of clients was large, it was difficult to make judgments about service level on a case-by-case basis. Applying the Pareto analysis, the total client base was divided into five groups. While these charts are for illustration purposes only and do not represent actual numbers or dollar figures for any specific company, they show how Pareto analysis can be used to aid in decision making.

The first chart shows the revenue produced by each client segment. It indicates that nearly twice the revenue is produced from segments A and B than from the remaining three segments. The second chart more clearly illustrates how service levels are being impacted. Not only are segments A and B producing significantly more revenue than the others, but the number of clients in those segments totals roughly 15 percent of the entire client base. The managers were then able to bring their service levels more in line with profitability and demand. The Pareto analysis also stimulated discussion about charges for services for each segment.

Pareto analysis differs from other types of analyses in its insistence on identifying the vital few. If an analysis is conducted and there does

Figure 11.7
Pareto Analysis

Revenue in $Millions			
Client Segment	2000	2001	2002	Average
Banks	$50.0	$60.0	$70.0	$60.0
Brokerage Houses	$40.0	$50.0	$60.0	$50.0
Insurance Companies	$20.0	$60.0	$30.0	$36.7
Independent Dealers	$10.0	$20.0	$30.0	$20.0
Everyone Else	$5.0	$5.0	$4.0	$4.7

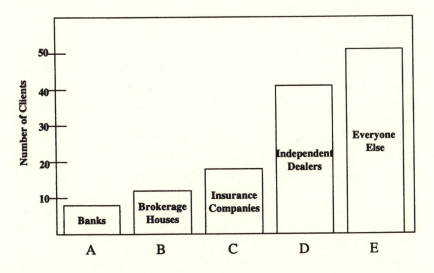

not appear to be any clearly defined 80-20 breakpoint, then it is most likely that the categories need to be reexamined and the data stratified in a different way.

LINK PIN DIAGRAM

A link pin diagram is useful for presenting and joining the assignable work activities. While it can be used in several configurations, it is included as a commitment diagram because specific responsibilities and even the names of those people charged with carrying out those responsibilities can be included in the diagram. The origin of the link pin idea comes out of decentralization studies done by human relations theorists including Rensis Likert, who used the link pin idea to propose that organizations should be structured around overlapping groups of employees instead of with independent divisions of the bureaucratic model. In Likert's model each subgroup is responsible for making decisions that affect its members.[5] However, one person would be assigned as a member of more than one subgroup. In this way each group could better understand the needs and problems of the other groups. Likert's model, however, deals with organizational structure rather than problem solving. The resulting diagram and much of the theoretical basis for it are useful for thinking through and illustrating task alignments and assignments.

Using the Tool

While link pin diagrams of various types can be used effectively at all stages of a discussion, they are particularly effective after the problems have been determined and the causes have been analyzed. A facilitator can use the link pin as a way of developing action plans and encouraging individuals to accept roles in completing those actions. Figure 11.8 illustrates a link pin diagram for the implementation of a new performance appraisal process. The goal is clearly stated on the top line with links drawn to the three key functional areas: Upper Management, Administration, and Training. In the best of circumstances, representatives from each of these functional areas are participating in the process. Further links are drawn from each functional area to specific tasks that need to be conducted by that area in order to achieve the desired result. If actual names can be assigned to each of the tasks, it is even better. Once the diagram is complete, it can be reexamined by the group to be sure that all aspects of the implementation have been covered. Perhaps new categories of involvement need to be developed. For example, if the output of the performance appraisal will be automated, perhaps there should be a functional role for the IT (Information Technology) department. In addition, the group may need some external support from a consultant to aid in the development of an appropriate and effective training program. The link pin both doc-

Figure 11.8
Link Pin Diagram

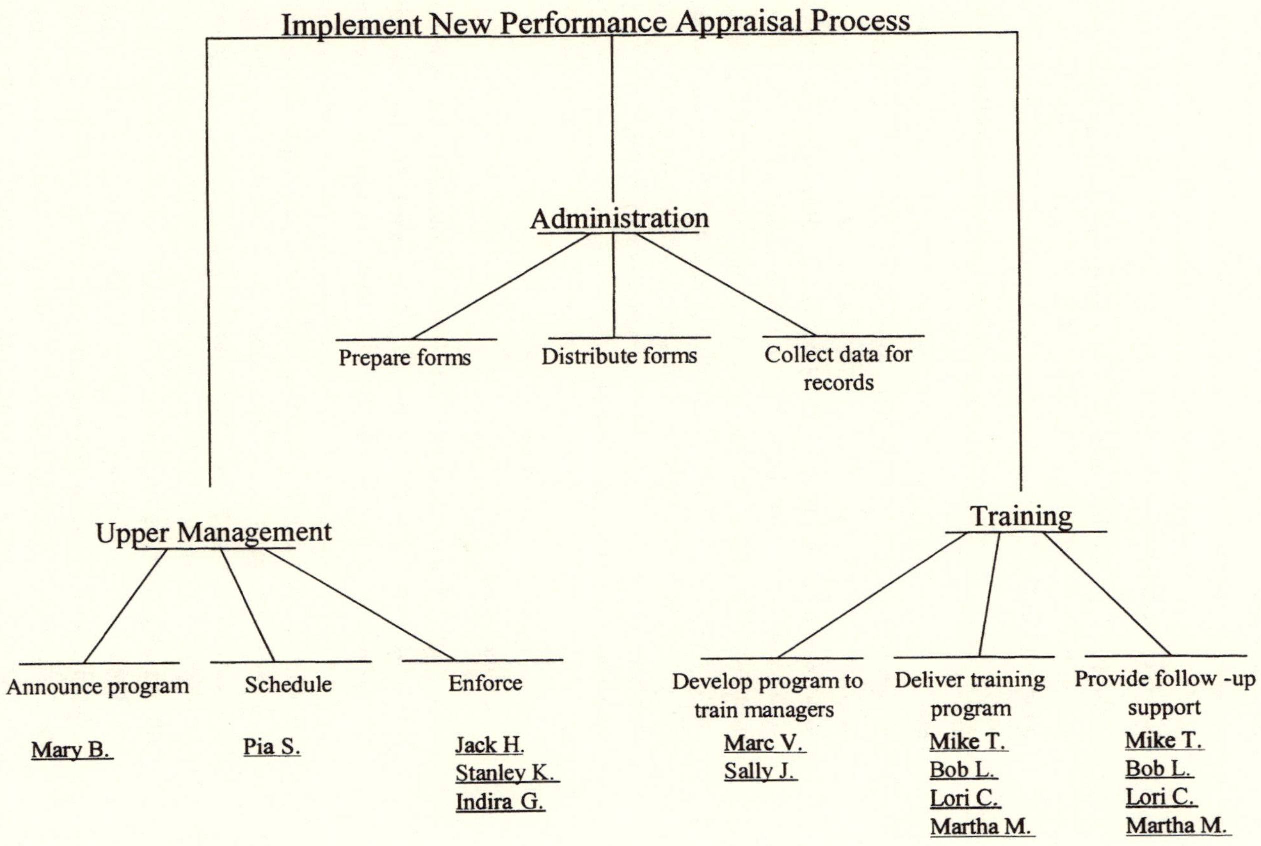

Implement New Performance Appraisal Process

Upper Management

- Announce program
  - Mary B.
- Schedule
  - Pia S.
- Enforce
  - Jack H.
  - Stanley K.
  - Indira G.

Administration

- Prepare forms
- Distribute forms
- Collect data for records

Training

- Develop program to train managers
  - Marc V.
  - Sally J.
- Deliver training program
  - Mike T.
  - Bob L.
  - Lori C.
  - Martha M.
- Provide follow-up support
  - Mike T.
  - Bob L.
  - Lori C.
  - Martha M.

uments the process and helps to keep the group from oversimplifying the problem.

GANTT CHART

In 1917 Henry L. Gantt, an American engineer and social scientist, developed a horizontal bar chart that bears his name. Using a Gantt chart allows the facilitator to develop and illustrate a schedule that helps to plan, coordinate, and track specific tasks in a project. Gantt charts are used as part of the commitment stage to represent the timing of tasks required to complete a particular project. Although in common usage as a project management tool, its usefulness as a discussion tool is often overlooked. When project schedules are developed with the full responsible group present, there is a greater likelihood that the time commitments will be kept. While Gantt charts give a very clear illustration of the project status, they don't indicate task dependencies. Because timing almost inevitably changes, Gantt charts developed during a meeting will be captured and formalized perhaps using one of the available electronic Gantt chart generators and updated by the manager, who then communicates the changes to the participants involved.

Using the Tool

A Gantt chart is constructed with a horizontal axis that represents the total time span of the project. This is further broken down into days, weeks, or months, as the case may be. On the vertical axis, the various milestones, or tasks to be completed, are listed. Horizontal bars are then drawn on the chart to represent the sequences, timing, and time span for each task. Time spans may overlap, thereby indicating that certain activities are taking place simultaneously. The chart shown in Figure 11.9 is an actual project plan created for the reengineering of the training process for a major insurance company done by our firm.

Often a Gantt chart will suggest areas of responsibility without specifically naming them. For example, in Figure 11.9 we see such things as "documents returned" and "compliance received." By the time a project gets to the Gantt chart stage, it is usually safe to assume that everybody understands whose responsibility it is to accomplish the tasks in the various time frames.

Figure 11.9
Gantt Chart

Project Development in Weeks (October 18, 1999 – February 25, 2000)

Tasks	1 10/18	2 10/25	3 11/1	4 11/8	5 11/15	6 11/22	7 11/29	8 12/6	9 12/13	10 12/20	11 12/27	12 1/3	13 1/10	14 1/17	15 1/24	16 2/7	17 2/14	18 2/21
Development of Training Design with Team				◄														
Instruction Group 1																		
• 1st draft to Team																		
-returned to TCPI					◄													
• 2nd draft to Business Partners																		
-returned to TCPI						◄												
• 3rd draft to Compliance								◄										
-returned to TCPI									◄									
Instruction Group 2																		
• 1st draft to Team																		
-returned to TCPI									◄									
• 2nd draft to Business Partners																		
-returned to TCPI											◄							
• 3rd draft to Compliance												◄						
-returned to TCPI													◄					
Instruction Group 3																		
• 1st draft to Team													◄					
-returned to TCPI													◄					
• 2nd draft to Business Partners														◄				
-returned to TCPI															◄			
• 3rd draft to Compliance																◄		
-returned to TCPI																	◄	
Finalize document and deliver to Client																		◄

NOTES

1. Jiro Kawakita, *KJ Method: A Scientific Approach to Problem Solving* (Tokyo: Kawakita Research Institute, 1975).

2. Kaoru Ishikawa, *What Is Total Quality Control?* (Englewood Cliffs, NJ: Prentice Hall, 1985).

3. Calvin S. Hall and Gardner Lindzey, *Theories of Personality*, 3rd ed. (New York: John Wiley & Sons, 1978).

4. A profile of Pareto and his theory can be found on the Web at http://www.economics.unimelb.edu.au/rdixon/pareto.html.

5. Rensis Likert, *New Patterns of Management*, ed. Arthur P. Brief (New York: Garland Publishing, 1987).

CHAPTER 12

Evaluating Group Performance

Evaluation of some kind should be part of every group encounter. In fact, whether as a facilitator or as a participant, we are continually making judgments about others in the group, the moment-to-moment effectiveness of what is being done, and the overall accomplishments of the total process. However, these judgments are most often held in private and therefore cannot be used to contribute to the growth and effectiveness of the group as a whole or its individual members. An important role for the facilitator is the stimulation and the surfacing of evaluative comments from the group and focusing these evaluations on continuous improvement of the group as a whole, the individual members, and the facilitator.

KEY CONCEPTS

- Evaluation and the role of commitment.
- Soliciting group feedback.
- Timing of evaluation.
- Resolving operational dysfunctions.
- Self-evaluation.

COMMITMENT AND SUCCESS

Overall positive group evaluations generally reflect that there was a positive outcome. This is most often hand in hand with a greater level of commitment. For individual participants a rewarding group experience enhances his or her commitment to the group's goals and decisions. Committed group members are more likely to promote activities that enhance cohesion, sacrifice personal gain for the good of the group, desire that membership in the group continue, and work for consensus instead of trying to win arguments. This principle has been studied extensively by Richard Moreland and John Levine.[1]

However, commitment means something more to the group than it does to the individual. When an individual is viewed positively by the group, there is a general willingness to expend energy to help that group member get through problems or to provide support for that group member's role when he or she is unable to attend. Moreland and Levine point out that in general the group demonstrates more acceptance of the individual's needs and values, maintains friendly ties, and is more likely to accommodate deviant behavior.[2] They go on to say that under normal conditions the commitment levels of the group and the individual are evenly matched. However, when they are not, they suggest that the "principle of least interest" applies.

The party that feels less committed has greater power in the relationship. If the group's level of the commitment greatly exceeds that of the individual, then he or she may come to occupy a position of status and authority within the group. In contrast, if an individual's level of commitment is greater than that of the group, then he or she will tend to have low power and may be derogated and devalued by other group members.[3]

Managers who facilitate need to take this into account. It seems to be an anomaly that someone with less commitment would have more power. However, in groups in which one member has little or no care or concern for the group or the consequences of a poor group performance, this phenomenon becomes apparent. When there is nothing at stake, a group member is free to do what he or she pleases. Unless there is some direct authoritative control of the deviant behavior, there is nothing the group can do that will matter to him or her. On the other hand, it is often apparent that the group takes advantage of a member that is too committed. That person is overburdened with an unfair share of the work and ultimately receives little of the credit. These people can be found at almost all levels in any organization. While they are significant individual contributors, it is difficult for them to move ahead, since promoting them means someone else must assume the burden of their work. Often these workers are candidates for burnout and either become ill or leave the organization in an effort at self-preservation.

Evaluating commitment on the part of individual members of a group is an ongoing necessity for facilitators. Where commitment discrepancies exist, a manager may have to address these issues "off-line" with the low-commitment individuals to determine what is causing the withholding of commitment and, where appropriate, to provide incentives and potential sanctions to raise the level of commitment. Evaluation can be seen as continuous and reciprocal. The group is continually evaluating individuals, while the individuals evaluate the benefits of their continued participation in the group. Some managers hold regular meetings because doing so makes them feel like they are managing. The participants find little value in these meetings but withhold criticism because of fear of sanction.

Most productive groups in organizational settings can be classified as task groups, which often evaluate members in terms of how well they help the group achieve its goals and enforce and conform to group norms. The individuals in these groups may judge the group in terms of such things as how much time the group demands, how much he or she enjoys the meetings, and his or her perception of the extent to which the group can satisfy personal interests and needs.

It is estimated that of the perhaps millions of meetings that take place worldwide every day, 99 percent of all groups ignore the evaluation process. Just the opposite should be the case. The only way groups can improve their efficiency and effectiveness is by opening up the process itself to scrutiny and feedback. When a group is not functioning well, most members are aware of the fact but choose to avoid dealing with it. Perhaps the feeling is that evaluating meetings may lead to spending time on further discussion that may not produce any tangible benefits. However, feedback aimed at preventing and eliminating ineffective practices can have very positive effects.

When evaluation of group process takes place, it is usually driven by the facilitator or by an outside process observer who has been assigned the task. All evaluation of group process must begin with an understanding of what needs to be observed and evaluated. Galanes and Brilhart provide us with a checklist consisting of questions in various categories to help structure a manager's thinking about evaluation during the planning and conducting stages as well as reflecting upon outcomes following a meeting (Figure 12.1).

Galanes and Brilhart are not recommending that every question on the list be answered; instead, they suggest using the list to screen out elements that seem to be working well so concentration can be placed on observing those that need improvement. Managers generally have the prerogative of providing feedback on process at any point during the meeting or after. However, feedback provided during the meeting should focus on such areas as keeping the subject on track and limiting discussion on issues that are either subordinate to the main purpose of the meeting or have been fully discussed already. Argument over process should be avoided unless the issue must be resolved before the group can move forward. Of course, any individual critical comments should be made to the members in question in private so that they will not feel attacked or publicly humiliated. In addition to feedback that may be required during the course of the meeting, it is my contention that the group should conduct an evaluation at the end of every meeting to monitor their practices and behaviors and answer two questions: How effective was this meeting? and What can we do to make the meeting better next time? Five minutes should be sufficient for this process, and the T account tool introduced below can be used as an effective instrument for collecting this feedback.

In addition to the feedback following each meeting, the manager may feel the need to further diagnose factors that are taking place that may be uncomfortable for individual members to surface during the feedback session. For this purpose, anonymous feedback instruments can be employed to allow group members to privately record their perceptions of the meeting and, in some cases, the facilitator as well.

The following evaluation instruments presented in this chapter have been selected based on my perception of what will work for managers. Managers are also encouraged to develop their own instruments that focus more specifically on their particular business or issues that are unique to the purpose and content of the discussions taking place.

T charts are a fundamental tool of any facilitation process. They can be used while conducting the meeting to point out comparisons and differences concerning the information that is forthcoming; they can help organize relationships between types of information or show opposite or opposing thinking on a particular issue; they can show a

Figure 12.1
Questions to Guide Your Observations

Group Goals

❑ Are there clear and accepted group goals?
❑ How well does the group understand its charge?
❑ Does the group know and accept limits on its area of freedom?
❑ Do members know what output they are supposed to produce?

Setting

❑ Does the physical environment (seating arrangements, privacy, attractiveness) facilitate group discussions?

Communication Skills and Interaction Patterns

❑ How clearly do members express their ideas and opinions?
❑ How well do members listen to each other?
❑ Do members complete one topic before they switch to another?
❑ Is verbal participation balanced equally among all members?
❑ Is the pattern of interaction all-channel or unduly restricted?

Communication Climate and Norms

❑ Does the group climate seem supportive and cooperative or defensive and competitive?
❑ What attitudes do the members exhibit toward themselves and each other?
❑ Do any hidden agenda items seem to interfere with group progress?
❑ Do any norms seem to interfere with group progress or cohesiveness?

Leadership and Member Roles

❑ What style of leadership is the designated leader providing?
❑ Is the leadership appropriate for the group's needs?
❑ Are the roles performed by members appropriate both for their skills and the needs of the group?
❑ Are there any needed functions not being provided by anyone?

Decision-Making and Problem-Solving Procedures

❑ Are members adequately prepared for meetings?
❑ Is the group using an agenda? If so, how well is it being followed? Does it serve the group's needs?
❑ Is anyone providing periodic internal summaries so members can keep track of major points of discussion?
❑ Are decisions, assignments, and proposals being recorded?
❑ How are decisions being made?

Figure 12.1 (continued)

❑   Has the group defined and analyzed the problem before members begin
    developing solutions?
❑   Do members understand and agree upon criteria in making decisions?
❑   How creative is the group in generating potential solutions?
❑   Are members deferring judgment until all solutions have been listed and
    understood?
❑   Do you see any tendency toward groupthink?
❑   Has the group made adequate plans to implement decisions?
❑   Are special procedures (brainstorming, problem census, etc.) being used as
    needed?
❑   Could procedural changes benefit the group?

Source: Gloria J. Galanes and John K. Brilhart, *Communicating in Groups: Applications
    and Skill*, 3rd ed. (Madison, WI: Brown & Benchmark, 1997), 282.

Figure 12.2
T Account

What went well?	Even better if . . .
• Full participation	• Avoid tangents and be more efficient with time
• Covered all the points on the agenda	• More time to prepare for the meeting so that all materials are available
• Action plan was developed	
• Everyone knows his/her responsibilities going forward	• Have an administrator attend the meeting to take notes

progression by listing an action plan on one side of the T and the timing
on the other. Figure 12.2 presents a T chart that I call the T account.
Its primary purpose is to account for what happened during the meeting
that was worthwhile and therefore should be retained, while at the same
time uncovering those components or processes that were unproductive
and therefore need modification. The headers placed at the top of each
column are a matter of personal preference. However, putting a positive
spin on the critical process may encourage a larger amount of candid
feedback. Use of the constructive criticism model stimulates more feedback by dealing with what went well first. In the example provided,
the meeting appears to have been quite successful, but several issues
around efficiency were raised. The facilitator can take these into ac-

Figure 12.3
Meeting Rating Scale

Characteristics	Excellent	Good	Average	Fair	Poor
Planning and Organization					
Equality of Participation					
General Cooperativeness					
Involvement and Listening to Understand					
Examination and Evaluation of Ideas					

Suggestions for future meetings:

_____

_____

_____

count for subsequent meetings. T accounts can be conducted in a very short period of time and add significant value to the facilitation process by addressing it directly. Also, when the manager facilitates using a T account at the end of the meeting, it raises his or her credibility and builds trust because of the demonstrated willingness to accept criticism.

ANONYMOUS EVALUATIONS

The quality of facilitation can be enhanced significantly by collecting postmeeting anonymous feedback from the group members. Depending on the needs of the situation, these instruments can be relatively simple or quite complex. Simple rating scales can be used by participants to evaluate all aspects of the meeting including group climate, cohesiveness, efficiency, satisfaction, freedom to express disagreement, and how well the discussion was organized. Figure 12.3 illustrates an all-purpose

Figure 12.4
IQARRC Facilitation Evaluation

Initiate	Began well and moved to new issues effectively					Ineffective beginning and drifted from topic to topic	
	7	6	5	4	3	2	1
Question	Controlled the discussion and stimulated participation					Random questions; no control	
	7	6	5	4	3	2	1
Actively Listen	High level of attention with frequent mirroring					Distracted with little feedback	
	7	6	5	4	3	2	1
Respond	Coordinated and synthesized key ideas					Had little to say or dominated the discussion	
	7	6	5	4	3	2	1
Resolve	Effectively handled argument and misunderstanding					Allowed the meeting to degenerate into conflict	
	7	6	5	4	3	2	1
Commit	Summarized the key points and created action plan					Issues unresolved; no one taking responsibility	
	7	6	5	4	3	2	1

discussion rating scale. Again, managers are encouraged to devise their own scales or modify some of those presented here to ensure that the evaluation is relevant to the content and circumstances of the meeting. Additional examples of postmeeting rating scales are included as Appendix C at the end of this book. It is useful for managers to periodically receive structured feedback on their performance as facilitators and leaders.

Figure 12.4, the IQARRC Facilitation Evaluation, asks participants to respond to questions relating to the six skill sets presented in this book. Data from this inventory can help a manager focus on those aspects of facilitating that need most attention. The IQARRC Facilitation Evaluation can also be used by the facilitator as a self-evaluation instrument. In fact, if the instrument is to be used for group feedback, it is recommended that the facilitator also fill out the instrument and compare the results. Discrepancies between the way the facilitator views his or her performance and the way the group views the same performance are subject to analysis and perhaps open discussion and can lead to both facilitator growth and improved overall group performance.

EVALUATION PRIOR TO GROUP INTERACTION

When departments or cross-functional teams will be meeting frequently and over a long period of time, the facilitator may want to gain some insight into potential benefits as well as challenges based on the interactive style that each member brings to the group. There are several standardized instruments on the market that will provide insight into the group's composition. In some cases it makes sense to acquire in-depth data on group interaction styles if the organization is willing to commit the time and resources to such a project. Meredith Belbin's Interplace might be considered. Belbin has been creating team role inventories for 20 years or more, and the latest version of his inventory, E-Interplace, can be conducted and scored on-line. It consists of a self-perception form and an observer form. The data from these forms are integrated with descriptions of job requirements and job observations, yielding a report that helps individuals and teams increase their understanding of themselves and others.[4]

Another instrument that I have used effectively with small groups is the Parker Team Player Survey. While this instrument yields far less complex data, it provides a good inventory of key behaviors that individuals bring with them to team activity. It is an excellent tool for stimulating discussion about group process and building awareness about how individual styles affect the dynamics of group performance. The Parker Team Player Survey also has two forms, one for the individual and the other to be completed by several people who interact with that individual in a group.[5]

The output of the survey identifies an individual as a contributor, collaborator, communicator, or challenger. Each of these categories is defined, and the score indicates the primary team player style. The primary style defines a set of behaviors used most often as a member of a team. It does not mean that it is the only style that is used or is accessible to each of the individuals. An awareness of the composition of the group by all of the members of that group allows conscious compensation for behaviors that are excessively present in the group or lacking. Also, when the facilitator understands the tendencies of a particular group, he or she can more effectively prepare for and manage the dynamics that will most likely occur in that group.

So we can see the important role that evaluation plays in helping the facilitator to observe, describe, and evaluate the group's performance.

Observations and evaluations can be conducted before, during, and after a particular meeting. Managers who want to be effective facilitators plan the evaluation process as part of the meeting and in fact include it on the agenda. When evaluation is presented consistently and in good faith, the group will rapidly accept it as an integral part of the overall process and as a key role they are expected to play in the enhancement of the group's performance.

NOTES

1. Richard Moreland and John Levine, "Socialization in Small Groups: Temporal Changes in Individual Group Relations," *Advances in Experimental Social Psychology* 15 (1982): 139.

2. Ibid., 137–192.

3. Ibid., 148.

4. E-Interplace can be accessed on-line at the Belbin Web site: http://www.belbin.com.

5. Glenn M. Parker, *Parker Team Player Survey* (Palo Alto, CA: Consulting Psychologists Press, 1991). Available online at http://www.cpp-db.com.

CHAPTER 13

Nonverbal Behavior in Groups

A fundamental skill for a facilitator is attending to and being able to interpret the feedback members of the group are providing moment to moment. In earlier chapters, we have discussed the issues centering around verbal communication that can impact the ability of the group to perform effectively. Understanding that the meaning of words lies within people rather than in the words themselves helps the savvy facilitator call for definitions and explanations as needed to ensure that the flow of communication and the meanings attached to it are relatively continuous. However, the overwhelming majority of all communication takes place on a nonverbal level. It has been estimated that 60 percent of the meaning of any personal message will be related to nonverbal communication.

KEY CONCEPTS

- Interpreting ambiguity in context.
- Distance as communication.
- Territoriality and group behavior.
- Reading body language.

While it is difficult enough to become astute at reading the nonverbal behavior of one individual with whom you might be communicating, the task is compounded when we consider the rich source of nonverbal messages being presented by groups simultaneously. By *nonverbal communication*, we mean creating meaning by using nonword symbols. Any symbol that is not specifically a word is automatically defined as nonverbal. These symbols can include gestures, objects, actions, and even the manner in which a word is presented.

Language has its limitations. So we rely on nonverbal behaviors to compensate for this inadequacy to express ourselves. Often nonverbal symbols are as carefully presented as verbal symbols, but they are much more difficult to keep under control. We sometimes show our true feelings with nonverbals whether or not we want to show them. Having said that, nonverbals are not precise, that is, they cannot be read exactly the same way with different people or in different contexts. The same gesture can have many meanings depending on the person using that gesture. Also, certain kinds of nonverbal communication are culture bound. A gesture of friendliness in one part of the world may be read as an insult in another.

One way of studying nonverbal communication is to break it into categories such as proxemics, kinesics, eye contact, facial expression, posture, tone of voice, and clothing. All of these categories communicate something about the individual, and this nonverbal communication tends to be more credible than the verbal messages. When a contradiction is observed between the verbal and the nonverbal, the tendency is to assign more truth to the nonverbal observation.

PROXEMICS

Proxemics is the study of the way humans (and animals) use space as symbolically significant behavior. Proxemics can be broken down into two additional parts: personal space and territoriality. Anthropologist Edward T. Hall defines four distances within which we communicate very specific intentions.[1] Hall's view is that we select various distances in relation to others based on how we feel toward the other person. The concept is an important one, even though Hall was describing North American reactions and other cultures may differ. Hall's distances incorporate the following:

• *Intimate distance*: The intimate zone begins with the skin and ranges out to about 18 inches. Within the group environment, the relative distances people establish between one another can signal close affiliation or distance, as the case may be. Even so, unless forced to meet in a closet, most groups would not exhibit intimate distances during a normal business meeting.

- *Personal distance*: The personal zone ranges from 18 inches to about 4 feet in length. Think of personal distance as being just beyond reach or "at arm's length." Groups that are very friendly and who have been working together for long periods of time will arrange themselves in personal distance relationships. The use of personal space is also an indication of the excitement level and the commitment of the group to the task at hand. Often the facilitator will see the group literally scoot their chairs closer together as they begin to work deeply into a problem.

- *Social distance*: The social zone ranges from about 4 to 12 feet out. Most one-to-one business conversations take place within social distance. However, the general arrangement of people around conference tables or in groups places some people closer together than others. This is important for the facilitator to note, since choices individuals make about whom to sit next to and whom to be the farthest from provide important clues into the dynamics of the group.

- *Public distance*: This zone runs outward from 12 feet and is generally not associated with group behavior. Public distance is more likely experienced in business situations such as a presentation, much as in a classroom setting.

Another phenomenon that can be observed is territoriality, which describes our need to establish and maintain a geographic area of our own. When a person becomes territorial, he or she assumes some kind of rights to a particular space. One of the interesting things about territoriality is the lack of basis for the assumption of any proprietary rights. In the case of groups that meet frequently, it can be observed that people will tend to occupy the same spaces. Individuals will often be visibly upset if their space has been occupied by someone else. Major changes in group dynamics can be achieved by simply rearranging the spaces and insisting that the group members occupy spaces that were not originally claimed as their territory.

While there is often no choice in the matter, the long rectangular or boat-shaped conference tables found in many offices and businesses do not provide the best arrangement for effective meetings. These tables make it difficult for group members to see all of the other members, and they contribute to uneven verbal participation. People sitting across from one another interact more than people sitting side by side or on the edges of each other's vision. If the facilitator has control over the setting for the meeting, he or she should select a round table where all members have easy eye contact with one another.

Eye contact can also be viewed as a spatial phenomenon. Since it signals that the channel for communication is open, avoiding eye contact generally means a person does not want to be called upon, while prolonged eye contact can signal either cooperativeness or competitiveness, depending upon the circumstances. Most Americans use eye contact before speaking and maintain it intermittently when conversing with someone they like. Other cultures may tend to avoid eye contact altogether or require unbreakable, continuous eye contact when conversing.

Eye contact and facial expressions present the whole range of emotions, including anger, sadness, happiness, support, disagreement, interest, and other responses that may occur in a group situation. An experienced facilitator will monitor the eye contact patterns and facial expressions occurring in the group for clues about individual responses to specific comments or the general climate of the discussion as a whole.

KINESICS

Kinesics is the study of bodily movement incorporating random motions, gestures, and a variety of involuntary physical responses that signal many feelings and attitudes. Body movement is an important part of all interpersonal interactions, and this holds true for groups as well. Like all nonverbals, body movements have an ambiguous quality and to some extent are culturally bound. Even so, an understanding of certain general concepts can be beneficial to effective facilitation. Some studies have shown that people turn directly toward others that they like and turn away from those that they dislike. They will also lean toward one another to indicate a sense of mutual inclusiveness, whereas leaning away might be a sign of rejection.[2]

Also, the concept of mirroring is very present in group interactions. When group members feel a sense of unity, they tend to imitate each others' posture and body movements. Members of the group who are experiencing tension may be observed swinging a foot, twisting a lock of hair, or tapping a pencil. While it may be difficult to discern exactly what may be causing this reaction, the facilitator needs to be alert to such movement and what might be causing it. When facilitating a group

Figure 13.1
Four Basic Body Positions

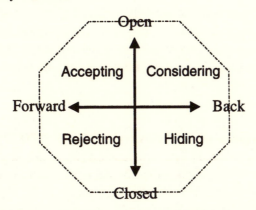

whose members are not well known to you, attentiveness to movement can indicate who has high status in the group. The group members are most likely to imitate the movements of high-status members. Also, high-status members tend to be the most relaxed, so they lean back and look around.[3]

FOUR BASIC BODY LANGUAGE POSITIONS

With so many things going on, a facilitator cannot focus entirely upon each individual's body language for protracted periods of time. However, some general observations may provide important data for additional scrutiny as the group dynamics develop. Take a quick inventory of the body positions adopted by members of the group. These positions will generally fall into four categories: open, closed, forward, or back. Figure 13.1 represents a simple positional model.

Once again, it is important to remember that body language is ambiguous. Therefore, reading and interpreting various positions and moves is not an exact science. An awareness of the possibilities of meaning associated with body positioning simply adds to the overall effectiveness of the facilitation process. So we might speculate that a person sitting with his or her arms folded, legs crossed, and body orientation turned away from the rest of the group is signaling some degree of rejection toward what is happening. Conversely, others fully facing the group with more open hand and leg positions may be illustrating acceptance.

Leaning forward or backward can be an indicator of the degree to which the participants are actively engaged in what is happening. A person leaning forward and actively engaged could either be accepting or rejecting what it is that is being said. Persons leaning back are illustrating a passive behavior that could be reflective of consideration of a point being made, or withdrawal or hiding from the activities taking place at the moment.

GESTURES

Research into gestures and their relationship to language has become quite complex and detailed. Much of the work being done on gestural communication goes beyond the facilitator's needs for effectively managing group process. Kendon classifies gestures along a continuum:

- *gesticulation*: idiosyncratic spontaneous movement of the hands and arms during speech
- *language-like gestures*: similar to gesticulation but grammatically integrated in the verbal messages
- *pantomime*: gestures without speech used in theatre to communicate a story
- *emblems*: "Italianate" gestures (e.g., insults and praises)
- *sign language*: a set of gestures and postures for a full-fledged linguistic communication system[4]

From the facilitator's point of view, there are three aspects of gesture that are important to consider.

1. Like all aspects of nonverbal communication, gestural signals are ambiguous. There is nothing absolute about interpreting a particular gesture because too many factors influence their meaning.
2. Gestural communication is generally automatic. In fact, the lack of gestures during communication in and of itself sends an ambiguous message.
3. When gestures and other nonverbal messages clash with what is being said, most people believe the truth is carried in the nonverbal signal. We call this clash a *disconfirming response*. Disconfirming responses often point to deception, hiding, or untruth on the part of the person exhibiting these behaviors. In an extreme example, one can envision a group member clenching his fist, turning red, and screaming at another group member, "No, I am not mad!"

READING NONVERBAL BEHAVIOR

Despite the ambiguities, there are certain clues that are provided through nonverbal communication that alert the facilitator to the various states of mind of the members of a group. Facial expression often belies what a person is truly feeling. This is because most of us know, at least unconsciously, that the face is the most obvious channel of expressing emotions. In business settings, people make a special effort to control what their faces might be telling others. On the other hand, because most people are less aware of the movement of their hands, legs, and feet, these movements provide a major source of information. While most body language is produced unconsciously, and may be nonspecific, some manifestations can be specific and repetitive. One senior executive with whom I worked for a relatively long period of time, during a coaching session, would slowly and systematically remove his pager, his watch, and his wedding ring and put them on the table in front of us. While I believe that these gestures were for the most part unconscious, I came to understand them as a signal, or an invitation, that all channels were open for discussion, including personal and professional issues, as they related to the work we were doing. Of particular significance was the gesture of removing the watch, thereby unplugging himself from his natural tendency to be driven by time.

Figure 13.2 lists some common body language behaviors and a possible interpretation for each. Again, it is important to note that all interpretations of body language must be done within a framework consisting of the context of the situation and your prior knowledge or experience with the individual.

SIGNALS TO PROBE FOR ADDITIONAL INFORMATION

One of the challenges of reading body language in a group situation is that the facilitator needs to assess each individual separately. Each person in the group brings a set of attitudes and risk issues associated with the subject of the meeting as well as the other members of the group.

Facilitators will often find it necessary to reach out to individual members to uncover hidden concerns or to draw them more closely to

Figure 13.2
Reading Nonverbal Behavior

Nonverbal Behavior	Interpretation
Arms crossed on chest	Defensiveness
Hand to cheek	Evaluation, thinking
Touching, slightly rubbing nose	Rejection, doubt, lying
Rubbing the eye	Doubt, disbelief
Hands clasped behind back	Anger, frustration, apprehension
Locked ankles	Apprehension
Rubbing hands	Anticipation
Hands clasped behind head, legs crossed	Confidence, superiority
Open palm	Sincerity, openness, innocence
Hands clenched or palms down	Defensiveness, withdrawal
Tapping or drumming fingers	Impatience
Patting/fondling hair	Lack of self-confidence, insecurity
Stroking chin	Trying to make a decision
Pulling or tugging at ear	Indecision

the group's mission or task. Here are some cues to focus observation on body language factors that require intervention.

Body position. Observe the body position of each person. If the position appears relaxed and stretched out, it may indicate the person is comfortable with the content and process of the meeting and is probably being open and truthful. On the other hand, if the legs and arms are held close to the body, it suggests that the person is keeping something in. Turning the head away or making a movement away from the facilitator or other group members may indicate reluctance to expand on some issues.

Hands. Observe the position and use of hands. When answering questions or providing information, are the palms up or down? Palms up suggests openness and cooperation. Palms down suggests defensiveness and may require a different approach to the subject or a need to probe for an underlying objection. A sudden move of one hand to the face is another indication of some discomfort with information or statements being provided. Sometimes this is as obvious as placing one or both hands in front of the mouth, often an indication that the person speaking doesn't believe what he or she is saying is the truth.

Generalized body movement. Watch for shoulder shrugging. The duration of a shrug is an important clue to someone's inner state. An extended shrug generally means ignorance or indifference. However, a quick or fleeting shrug suggests that the person is trying to appear relaxed and casual when the opposite is true.

All individual gestures need to be observed in relation to what's being said. Sometimes gestures for emphasis look forced or lack spontaneity. Emotional responses like surprise generally come and go quickly. If they are prolonged, they raise the suspicion of deceit.

RESPONDING TO NONVERBAL BEHAVIOR

Managing and responding to nonverbal behavior begins with an understanding that nonverbal communication primarily expresses attitudes. Hopefully, if the meeting is purposeful and has been structured well, the nonverbal behavior will express interest, liking, support, commitment, and other behaviors that indicate group cohesiveness. However, it is also likely that periodically nonverbal behavior will express disagreement, anxiety, rejection, and other states of mind that are potentially damaging to the achievement of the group's mission.

When negativity is observed through the body language of one or more group members, it needs to be addressed in one of two ways. The first option calls for making note of the behavior and when it occurred during the meeting. Having details at hand enables the facilitator to stimulate remembrance on the part of the individual or individuals involved. As soon as possible following the meeting the person or persons should be spoken to privately regarding the observation. Managers need to be particularly careful to remain neutral and withhold judgment in order to ensure the willingness of the person to express the concerns that generated the body language in question.

The second approach calls for addressing the observation at the time of occurrence during the meeting. Again, a judgment needs to be made whether opening up the observation to discussion would create undo pressure or defensiveness on members of the group. However, having observed several members of the group sitting back with their arms folded and being generally nonresponsive, the facilitator would probably do well to address the underlying issue before trying to move on.

Once during a working session with a group of advertising executives concerning presentation meetings, one participant offered the following story:

He was about one third of the way through his presentation when the senior person on the client side stood up, picked up her chair, turned around her chair, and sat back down. This was very disconcerting and made it very difficult for him to continue with enthusiasm.

I asked him, "What did you do?"

He said, "I finished the presentation as quickly as I could."

Somewhat incredulously, I asked, "Why?"

He said, "Because I had more slides."

The fact is that such a strong nonverbal signal on the part of a high-status person in the group indicates that no forward progress can be made until the immediate issue is addressed. There is a strong tendency, however, to continue moving in the same direction in the hope that momentum, or some subsequent information or event, will save the day. What is actually called for here is a major shift in the subject of the discussion from content to process.

CONTENT-PROCESS SHIFT

The content-process shift is an assertiveness technique that can be used very effectively in a group situation. The content-process shift operates on the premise that communication is always taking place on two levels. One level is the content or substance of what is being communicated. The other level is the process or how something is being communicated. The vast majority of all communication focuses on content. A facilitator may elect to use a content-process shift when one or more of the following situations occur:

• There is a sense that something is wrong.
• The conversation dies.
• Questions go unanswered.
• The facilitator or members of the group are becoming defensive or angry.
• The facilitator feels like withdrawing.

By shifting the discussion from content to process, the facilitator can uncover hidden objections, focus on what's happening rather than what's being said, provide an option to withdraw, and build trust through self-disclosure. For example, in our previous scenario, perhaps the account executive would have been better served at the time the client turned her chair around to say something like, "I am getting a very clear indication that something contained in my presentation or the way I am presenting it is not being received in the manner I intended. Can we discuss what I may be able to do to put us back on track?"

While there is no guarantee that the account executive would have received a positive response, the possibility exists that the shift from content to process might have opened up a dialogue focused on the underlying concerns of the client. Often by focusing on process and getting people to discuss the factors that are upsetting them or raising objections, the facilitator has an opportunity to manage those objections or adjust to the concerns being raised. Managers in particular need to continuously probe for underlying feelings and risk issues, while at the same time assuring the participants that it is safe to express their concerns. The ability of a manager to demonstrate a sensitivity to the feeling and tone of group process as well as the content and substance of the discussion goes a long way toward supporting the perception of that manager as a leader.

Group dynamics involves both verbal and nonverbal messages. While we can hope that verbal messages are for the most part clear and acceptable to others in a group situation, along with the context of the situation, verbal messages can sometimes communicate and generate undesirable emotions. Nonverbal communication is continuous and carries a great deal of meaning. Where words are used to express ideas, nonverbal behaviors most often convey attitudes and emotions. They provide excellent data to assist in managing group process, but nonverbal messages should be interpreted with caution since they are usually ambiguous and are often culture bound.

NOTES

1. Edward T. Hall, *The Hidden Dimension* (Garden City, NY: Anchor, 1969), 160–161.

2. A.E. Scheffler, "Quasi-Courtship Behavior in Psychotherapy," *Psychiatry* 28 (1965): 245–256.

3. Judee K. Burgoon and Thomas Saine, *The Unknown Dialogue: An Introduction to Nonverbal Communication* (Boston: Houghton Mifflin, 1978).

4. Adam Kendon, "Gesticulation and Speech: Two Aspects of the Process of Utterance," in *The Relationship of Verbal and Nonverbal Communication*,

ed. Mary Ritchie Key (The Hague: Mouton, 1980), 207–227; and Adam Kendon, "How Gestures Can Become Like Words," in *Cross-Cultural Perspectives in Nonverbal Communication*, ed. Fernando Poyatos (Toronto: Hogrefe, 1988), 131–141; also "Gesture" in *Annual Review of Anthropology* 26 (1997): 109–128.

CHAPTER 14

The Ethics of Facilitation

At various points in this book, we have talked about the need for managers to build trust. In Chapter 3, we looked at the components of leadership and outlined three core competencies that define what a leader is: consistency, commitment, and courage. This discussion of ethics is included here because the book addresses managers in particular as well as facilitators both inside and outside the organization in nonmanagement roles.

KEY CONCEPTS

• Ethics defined.
• The manager's ethical dilemma.
• The amorality of ethical decisions.

Managers face many ethical decisions on a daily basis. At the time this book was being prepared, some of the largest and most valued corporations in America are coming under scrutiny or are in fact in total disarray based on the perceived violation of ethical business practices. Successful managers for the long term are those that establish trust and integrity in their working relationships.

One cannot discuss the subject of ethics relating to facilitation without examining business and professional ethics in general. Funk and Wagnalls' *New Comprehensive Dictionary of the English Language* defines *ethics* as "the study and philosophy of human conduct, with emphasis on the determination of right and wrong."[1] *Ethical* is defined as "in accordance with right principles as defined by a given system of ethics or professional conduct." It is not our purpose here to rehash the systematic practices of illegal actions by major organizations that have been reported on over the last 25 years. However, some estimates suggest that between 1975 and 1985 alone two thirds of the Fortune 500 firms were convicted of serious crimes ranging from price fixing to illegal dumping of hazardous wastes.[2] More recently, major financial institutions, insurance, and energy companies have continued to be the target of serious investigations into improprieties and continue to pay substantial monetary and criminal penalties for acknowledged wrongdoing. The incidents surrounding the Enron debacle, Worldcom, Tyco, and Andersen's role continue to unravel as this manuscript is being prepared. However, the toll on individual lives in terms of loss of employment and loss of life savings has been devastating.

While much has been, and will continue to be, written about organizational ethics and the problems associated with achieving a high standard, some research indicates that upper management rarely communicates a clear set of values to the employees. Read through any organization's statement of values and you will see wording that is highly abstract or internally inconsistent. They may serve to lessen the legal liability of upper management; however, they provide the employees with little guidance. Phrases like "fair and equitable treatment" and "responsiveness to the customer" appear frequently, but they provide little guidance when the needs of a small customer or a low-power colleague are shifted to the back burner in favor of the demands of more powerful people.

With this as a backdrop, we turn our attention to the way managers interact with the groups of people in their charge. The formulation of human resource policies with an eye toward trying to provide a rational and fair way of dealing with people in the organization, more often than not, provides guidelines for managers on what they cannot do rather than on actually helping them deal with individuals and get things done. Rules created by bureaucracies relate to abstract categories that dictate how people are to be treated regardless of individual circumstances. They rarely take into account types of relationships, individual differences, idiosyncratic characteristics, or unusual circumstances.[3]

Marvin Weisbord has argued strongly that the more influence people have over their jobs, the more motivated, productive, and healthy they are. He agrees with Marshall Sashkin that participative management is an ethical imperative. "Low control of their own work hurts people physically and emotionally," wrote Sashkin. "[T]herefore ethical managers should not knowingly reduce people's control by excluding them from important matters that affect them."[4]

It is easy enough to say that ethical decisions should be a matter of black or white and that managers should continually act in ways that would be above reproach based upon the highest standards available. Yet everything that we know about organizations suggests that bureaucratic structure inherently transfers ethical responsibility from individuals within the organization to the organizational structure. In this manner, ethical responsibility is perceived as being shared by many people in the organization, or the responsibility is perceived as being assumed by a "higher power" in the organization, thus creating a "just following orders" syndrome. The culture of the organization also often discourages the discussion of ethical issues, or as Toffler concluded sometime ago, "There seems to be a sense among managers that talking about ethics is 'just not done here,' and unfortunately they are usually right."[5]

These cultural attitudes and variables affect the way the manager conducts himself or herself in the day-to-day process of meeting with and managing people in the organization. My belief, derived from over 30 years of practice in various organizational settings, leads me to the conclusion that most managers have an ethical bias; that is, they would prefer to do "the right thing." Many managers are haunted for their entire professional lives by a decision they feel they were forced to make based on organizational considerations that fell outside of their personal ethical framework. It is not the intention of this book to draw hard boundaries between what might be considered ethical behavior in managing group process and those behaviors that could be considered unethical. It falls to each individual to make his or her own choices in this regard. At best, a suggestion of some guidelines to help in this decision process may be appropriate.

One of the challenges is that most managers believe that their jobs require them to compromise their own values. A study by Posner and Schmidt found that 72 percent of employees feel that they face pressure to engage in actions they consider unethical. Approximately 41 percent of those managers admit that they have bowed to pressure and acted in ways contrary to their values.[6]

The following two scenarios relate specifically to group process and present the managers involved with what I consider to be ethical dilemmas.

SITUATION 1

The head of a major business unit is given the task to facilitate the development of a new product with relatively short turnaround time. The product is to be developed by a department within the business unit that is targeted for elimination relatively soon after the new product hits the market. The manager is provided incentives in the form of a substantial bonus and larger responsibility based on her performance in accomplishing this task.

In taking up the challenge, the manager facilitates a number of meetings including off-sites during the next several months. She incorporated several motivational elements in the process including team-building and strategic planning exercises supporting the notion that the fortunes of this department would rise on the successful completion of this task and the potential for a bright future was at hand. The department tackled the problems enthusiastically, meeting deadlines that required extensive flexibility in time and resources.

In the end, the product was completed on time and was deemed to be a great success, and a party was held to celebrate everyone's good fortune. One month later, the department was closed and all of the people were fired.

SITUATION 2

Facing increasing competition and feeling the effects of an economic downturn, this company finds itself in an almost continuous state of reorganization. Every few months, departments and responsibilities are realigned, and reductions in force are mandated in a continual process of lowering expenses. The manager of a large department on the technical side of the organization is faced increasingly with productivity and morale issues and the ability of his organization to deliver essential services to both internal and external clients. Despite knowing full well that further reorganization and personnel cuts will be coming down the line, the manager embarks on an ambitious program of visioning and strategic planning. He facilitates a number of off-site meetings with his direct reports and managers one level below his direct reports, with the purpose of engaging everyone in a project that focuses on the future and provides a structured forum for them to discuss their concerns. The output from these meetings consists of a comprehensive business plan as well as several specific action items with assigned responsibility. Within a matter of weeks following these sessions, another reorganization was announced. Responsibilities were once again realigned, and several of the participants including two of the direct reports were fired.

What can we say about these managers? Can they be indicted for using the facilitation process in an unethical manner? Or is facilitation to be seen as simply another tool for managers to achieve individual and organizational ends regardless of the consequences for the individuals who apply their collective efforts in good faith to achieve a goal? Some people might say that the first situation demonstrates more unethical behavior because the group in question is consciously misled into believing they have a future that doesn't really exist. However, it is also possible to say the same for the second situation, since although not overtly stated, the futures of many of the participants in Situation 2 were equally tenuous. Can we resolve the issue by pointing to the fact that in Situation 1 the manager seems to be acting primarily out of self-interest, achieving her bonus and a larger piece of the pie, while in the second situation the manager appears to be primarily concerned with benefits that would accrue to the organization through his facilitation efforts?

Any discussion of ethics particularly when applied to situations that incorporate a great deal of ambiguity is bound to raise as many questions as it answers. The guidelines offered here are provided for managers to raise questions about their own ethical boundaries and promote the perception that they are in fact operating on an ethical basis.

- Ethical managers should not knowingly reduce people's control by excluding them from important matters that affect them. After its introduction in the 1980s, participative management was perceived by some theorists as an ethical imperative. This was built on evidence showing that the more influence people have over their jobs, the less likely they are to be physically ill, let alone demotivated and unproductive.

- The ethical manager balances the three major types of ethical norms: standards that describe the manager's qualifications and values; principles, which describe the manager's responsibilities; and rules, which describe the boundaries of the individual's duties, obligations, and behaviors. When one describes an effective manager or, for that matter, an effective leader, it is not uncommon to hear that person described in terms of their adherence to high standards and certain absolutes. A principle that is fundamental to effective facilitation is to always treat people as ends, never only as means, to respect their individuality and never use them only for their ability to do things.

- Ethical managers use groups to help make decisions rather than rubber-stamp decisions that have already been made. Meetings should not give the illusion of participative decision making when management's mind is already made up.

- Ethical managers sell the virtues of participation and do not force employees to participate in a process against their will. Associated with this would be the drawing into a group employees who really don't know what they are getting into.

We began this chapter highlighting the importance of trust, and we will end on the same note. How does a manager go about building trust? He or she does so by communicating clearly and honestly, by making and keeping realistic promises, adhering to confidentiality, and treating everyone with the respect they deserve. A manager cannot be effective if his or her staff or other coworkers feel a lack of integrity. Here are some general ethical considerations for managers that can be applied to facilitation. The following list is selected and adapted from *The Successful Manager's Handbook*.[7]

- Make promises only if you plan to keep them.
- Be willing to openly discuss ethical issues.
- Follow up with those who question your decisions to understand their concerns and to explain the reasons for your decisions.
- Model your ethical beliefs through your behavior.
- Seek feedback on others' perceptions of your honesty and ethics.
- Be authentic; seek opportunities to strengthen your self-insight and then share who you are and what you believe and feel.
- Adhere to your company's written code of ethics and apply it judiciously.

- Don't promise confidentiality if you are not certain you can keep the information private.
- Stand up for others, especially for your people when they need your support.
- If you receive feedback that you are seen as untrustworthy or unethical, seek clarification, avoid defensiveness, and work to understand the other person's point of view.

Some sincere effort has been put into developing a code of ethics for facilitators in general. The International Association of Facilitators (IAF) established a working group called the IAF Ethics and Values Think Tank (EVTT), which began work in June 2000 and completed a draft statement in May 2002. The process leading to the "IAF Statement of Values and Code of Ethics" involved an estimated 150 people. According to the IAF, an on-line group of 85 people exchanged more than 900 e-mails and engaged in thousands of thinking and discussion hours on the EVTT E-group. In addition, two forums involving 40 people were held at the IAF Conference 2001 at Minnesota. Workshops and discussions were also held at regional conferences and on regional e-groups. A complete copy of the "Draft Statement of Values and Code of Ethics for Facilitators" is included as Appendix D. However, some elements of the draft statement are worth highlighting here.

The following from the section "Statement of Values" should apply to managers who facilitate as well as facilitation professionals.

As group facilitators, we believe in the inherent value of the individual and the collective wisdom of the group. We strive to help the group make the best use of the contributions of each of its members. We set aside our personal opinions and support the group's right to make its own choices. We believe that collaborative and cooperative interaction builds consensus and produces meaningful outcomes.[8]

A manager who doesn't share the belief that the group has the right to make its own choices and that consensus produces meaningful outcomes should not bother to hold meetings at all, just give orders. This statement from the section "Respect, Safety, Equity, and Trust" also provides an ethical basis for management facilitation: "We strive to engender an environment of respect and safety where all participants trust that they can speak freely and where individual boundaries are

honoured. We use our skills, knowledge, tools, and wisdom to elicit
and honour the perspectives of all."[9]

In addition to these principles, a manager needs an awareness of the
visible and invisible differences within his or her group. In his or her
role as a facilitator, he or she must ensure that the entire group respects
those differences. It also falls to the manager to ensure that group members feel valued and significant. As much as possible, everyone in the
group should be made to feel that they have some measure of power
despite the relative inequities of their positions. One aspect of power
within the group that needs to be managed is the power certain members may experience because of their relationship with the manager.
There is a natural tendency, unless controlled, to acknowledge and support those members of the group who have a closer relationship with
the manager or have previously demonstrated their support for the manager's points of view.

Responding ethically is a two-way street. While the manager should
be expected to present honest and accurate information, he or she
should also expect that information shared by group members is like-
wise honest and accurate. Any behavior not meeting these standards
must be called into question, and sanctions should be imposed. Managers should assert that this behavior is not acceptable within the group
and of course should refrain from using these behaviors themselves.

NOTES

1. Funk & Wagnalls, *New Comprehensive International Dictionary of the
English Language* (Newark, NJ: Publishers International Press, 1982), 436.

2. M. Moser, "Ethical Conflict at Work," *Journal of Business Ethics* 7
(1988): 381–387.

3. Carol Heimer, "Doing Your Job and Helping Your Friends: Universalistic
Norms about Particular Others in Networks," in *Networks and Organizations:
Structure, Form and Action*, ed. Nitin Nohria and Robert G. Eccles (Boston:
Harvard Business School Press, 1992), 247–265.

4. Marvin R. Weisbord, *Productive Workplaces: Organizing and Managing
for Dignity, Meaning, and Community* (San Francisco: Jossey-Bass, 1989), 169.

5. Barbara Ley Toffler, *Tough Choices: Managers Talk Ethics* (New York:
John Wiley, 1986), 337.

6. B.Z. Posner and W.H. Schmidt, "Values and the American Manager,"
California Management Review 26 (1984): 202–216.

7. Brian L. Davis, Carol J. Skube, Lowell W. Hellervik, Susan H. Gebelein,

and James L. Sheard, *The Successful Manager's Handbook: Development Suggestions for Today's Managers* (Minneapolis: Personnel Decisions, Inc., 1992), 583–584.

8. International Association of Facilitators, "The International Association of Facilitators Draft Statement of Values and Code of Ethics for Facilitators," IAF Web site, http://www.iaf-world.org/iafethicsTT.htm.

9. Ibid., "Respect, Safety, Equity, and Trust."

Appendix A:
Example Agenda for Visioning Meeting

Day One

9:00   Greetings and Introductions

- Manager initiates program and gives statement of support for the action planning process and speaks on the goals and objectives of the division and on his vision of what the team should accomplish during the session and beyond.
- Short Q&A on positioning of the division within organization, upper management support, and so on.

9:30   Meeting Objectives

- The facilitator (M. Gottlieb) outlines the objectives and the events that will take place during the session.

9:45   The Ideal 2002

- Participants are grouped as departments.
- The department's task is to make a list of "ideal" circumstances, considering factors such as:
  —customer focus
  —service goals
  —staff deployment goals
  —reorganization goals
  —teamwork goals
  —personal and professional goals
- Each department reports its results to the large group. (30 min.)

10:45   Break

11:00   The Real 2002

- Participants return to department groups.

- They contrast the ideal situation with the current situation, for example, "What's happening now?" (30 min.)

- They examine the gap between the ideal and the real and rank their ability to impact the issue: A—We have a high degree of control to change this condition; B—We have some control and the ability to influence changes in this condition; or C—We have little or no control or influence regarding this condition. (15 min.)

- Participants take a "museum walk"; that is, each group walks around the room, reviewing each of the other groups' flip charts and examining the groups' output. (15 min.)

12:00   Lunch

1:00   Team Player Survey

- Facilitator shares results of the Team Player Survey, pointing out which roles are abundant and those that need more attention.

- Some basics of group process are introduced.

1:30   Creative Problem Solving

- The group is challenged to solve some standard creative problem-solving puzzles.

- Some strategies for employing creative problem solving are discussed.

2:00   Space Tower

- Participants are grouped as departments.

- The groups are challenged with a team-building exercise that requires them to plan, organize, develop a budget, and construct a "space tower" using Tinker Toys.

3:15   Break

3:30   Build the Tower

- The groups compete with each other by building their towers and trying to meet the criteria they set for themselves in terms of height, number of pieces, stability, and time taken to build.

- The discussion following the exercise covers elements of group formation: how groups approach a task, group roles, and other group dynamics.

4:00   Answering Concerns

- Participants are grouped (as departments or some other logical division) and asked to develop questions for the manager such as but not limited to:
  —his vision for the organization
  —his preferred work style
  —how best to communicate with him
  —his general expectations for his direct reports
  —his views on general company issues
- These questions are placed on note cards and collected by the facilitator, who will consolidate duplicates or ask the groups for clarification if necessary.

4:30   Wrap-up Discussion

5:00   Adjourn

Day Two

9:00   Overview of Day 2

9:15   Responding to concerns (manager)

- The facilitator asks the manager the questions generated by the groups.

10:15   Break

10:30   Developing Business and Action Plans

- Participants are returned to their departmental groups.
- They revisit the gap analysis they prepared on Day 1.
- Each department develops a business plan by responding to the following template:
  —trends and goals that will impact the department
  —the mission/purpose of the department
  —the department's client base
  —service goals and objectives
  —staffing structure
  —staffing roles and responsibilities
  —interdependencies with other departments
  —future planning: goals and objectives

12:00   Lunch

1:00   Business Plan Presentation
         • Each group presents its business plan.
         • The output is consolidated into a business plan for the entire organization.

2:00   Group Juggling
         • Participants engage in a team-building and communication exercise.

2:45   Break

3:00   Developing Communication among Departments
         • Department groups discuss needs and wants for contracting with other departments and senior management.
         • The groups create a visual map of their communication needs and interdependencies with other departments
         • The maps are displayed and explained.

4:30   General Discussion, Q&A, Wrap-up

5:00   Adjourn

Appendix B:
Facilitation Planning Kit

PREPARATION

Today's Date: *mm/dd/yy*

Meeting Date: *mm/dd/yy*

Meeting Purpose:

What is the purpose for calling the meeting?

_____

_____

Is a meeting the best format to achieve your purpose? (Yes/No) If answering no, what is a better strategy?

_____

_____

Meeting Type

What kind of meeting are you preparing?

Information giving
Fact finding
Problem solving
Persuading
Training
Decision making

Participant List

Who are the participants and what value does each bring to the subject matter?

What is each participant expected to contribute to the meeting? Each person should know why he or she has been selected to attend; e.g., particular information or expertise.

Participant	Title/function	Value

Meeting Objectives

What are the *critical success factors/desired outcomes*? By the end of the meeting, what do you and the group want to have achieved?

_____

_____

_____

_____

Are there additional *learning objectives*? If so, what are they? Are there things you want the participants to learn that would help them function better together?

_____

_____

_____

_____

Participant and Group Issues

What assumptions can you make about this group and this particular meeting? What are some individual or group issues/problems for which you should prepare?

It is important to anticipate the group's behavior before designing an agenda.

_____

_____

_____

_____

What are your contingency plans if problems develop?

_____

_____

_____

_____

Meeting Length

What is your initial estimate about how much time is required for the meeting?

_____

_____

_____

_____

Premeeting Tasks

Facility arrangements

Location: _____

Room size: _____

Cost estimates: _____

Seating/table
arrangement: _____

Equipment arrangements

	Overhead projector/screen
	LCD
	VCR/monitor
	Flip charts
	White board
	Conference calling

Additional arrangements

	Memo to participants
	Organize information
	Distribute information prior to meeting
	Confirm attendance

THE MEETING

Meeting Strategy

Review the meeting's purpose and objectives, your assumptions, the group's makeup, and issues. What would be a general strategy for achieving the objectives?

_____

_____

_____

_____

Meeting Activities

List the activities needed for each phase of the meeting. Estimate how long each activity will take. This section allows the facilitator some freedom to brainstorm ideas before developing a specific agenda.

Phase I: Opening

_____

_____

_____

_____

Phase II: Middle

_____

_____

_____

_____

Phase III: Ending

_____

_____

_____

_____

Tools and Techniques

Which tools and techniques will support the meeting activities?

Choose from the array of tools and techniques that can help you conduct the meeting efficiently and effectively.

_____

_____

_____

_____

The Agenda

Using the following format, write a final version of the desired outcomes and develop a detailed agenda.

Desired Outcomes:

_____

_____

_____

Agenda Format:

Time	Activity	Person	Desired Outcome

Roles and Responsibilities

What are participant natural roles, or which assignments need to be made?

- Group Leader: _____

- Facilitator: _____

- Recorder: _____

- Presenters: _____

- Timekeeper: _____

- Follow-up: _____

Meeting Ground Rules

If the group has not established meeting ground rules, be prepared to discuss this and help them generate a list. Be prepared with a list of your own in order to start the discussion.

_____

_____

_____

_____

Supplementary Tools for Planning

It may be useful to employ some tools that help develop or expand sections of the Planning Kit. Here are a few that managers may find helpful in keeping them focused and covering all the bases.

Tool Selection Checklist

Data Collection

- What data exist?
- Do we need more data?
- How should the data be collected?

Data Analysis

- How are the data organized?
- What type of analysis should be applied to the data?
- Do the data need to be grouped or organized in a specific manner?
- Is there a tool that can help facilitate analysis of these data?
- Can the outcomes of analysis be mapped visually?

Presentation

- Are the data and subsequent analysis easy to understand?
- Are the relationships between various components clearly discernible?
- How can we put our analysis into action?

Consideration of these questions will lead the facilitator toward selecting tools and processes that help ensure understanding among all group members and produce results.

Appendix C:
Postmeeting Rating Scales

PROBLEM-SOLVING PROCESS RATING SCALE

Poor	Fair	Average	Good	Excellent
1	2	3	4	5

Circle the appropriate number in front of each item.

1 2 3 4 5   (1) The concern of each member was identified regarding the problem the group attempted to solve.

1 2 3 4 5   (2) This concern was identified *before* the problem was analyzed.

1 2 3 4 5   (3) In problem analysis, the present condition was carefully compared with the specific condition desired.

1 2 3 4 5   (4) The goal was carefully defined and agreed to by all members.

1 2 3 4 5   (5) Valid (and relevant) information was secured when needed.

1 2 3 4 5   (6) Possible solutions were listed and clarified before they were evaluated.

1 2 3 4 5   (7) Criteria for evaluating proposed solutions were clearly identified and accepted by the group.

1 2 3 4 5   (8) Predictions were made regarding the probable effectiveness of each proposed solution, using the available information and criteria.

1 2 3 4 5   (9) Consensus was achieved on the most desirable solution.

1 2 3 4 5   (10) A detailed plan to implement the solution was developed.

1 2 3 4 5   (11) The problem-solving process was systematic and orderly.

Source: Gloria J. Galanes and John K. Brilhart, *Communicating in Groups: Applications and Skills*, 3rd ed. (Madison, WI: Brown and Benchmark, 1997), 392.

POSTMEETING REACTION FORM

Circle the number that best indicates your reactions to the following questions about the discussion in which you participated.

1. *Effectiveness of communication.* To what extent do you feel members were understanding each others' statements and positions?

0	1	2	3	4	5	6	7	8	9	10

Talked past each other; misunderstanding

Communicated directly with each other and understanding

2. *Opportunity to participate.* To what extent did you feel free to speak?

0	1	2	3	4	5	6	7	8	9	10

Never had a chance

Had all the opportunity I wanted

3. *Climate of acceptance.* How well did members support each other, show acceptance of individuals?

0	1	2	3	4	5	6	7	8	9	10

Highly critical and punishing

Supportive and receptive

4. *General climate.* How pleasant and concerned were members with interpersonal relations?

0	1	2	3	4	5	6	7	8	9	10

Quarrelsome, status differences emphasized

Pleasant, empathic, concerned with persons

5. *Leadership.* How effective was the leader (or leadership) of the group?

0	1	2	3	4	5	6	7	8	9	10

Too weak or dominating   Group-centered and focused

6. *Satisfaction with role.* How satisfied are you with your personal participation in the discussion?

0	1	2	3	4	5	6	7	8	9	10

Very dissatisfied   Very satisfied

7. *Quality of product.* How satisfied are you with the discussions, solutions, or learnings that came out of this meeting?

0	1	2	3	4	5	6	7	8	9	10

Very displeased   Very satisfied

8. *Overall.* How do you rate the meeting as a whole apart from any specific aspect of it?

0	1	2	3	4	5	6	7	8	9	10

Awful; waste of time   Superb; time well spent

Source: Adapted from Gloria J. Galanes and John K. Brilhart, *Communicating in Groups: Applications and Skills*, 3rd ed. (Madison, WI: Brown and Benchmark, 1997), 295.

213

SEASHORE INDEX OF GROUP COHESIVENESS

Check one response for each question.

1. Do you feel that you are really a part of your work group?

    ___ Really a part of my work group
    ___ Included in most ways
    ___ Included in some ways, but not in others
    ___ Don't feel I really belong
    ___ Don't work with any one group of people
    ___ Not ascertained

2. If you had a chance to do the same kind of work for the same pay in another work group, how would you feel about moving?

    ___ Would want very much to move
    ___ Would rather move than stay where I am
    ___ Would make no difference to me
    ___ Would want very much to stay where I am
    ___ Not ascertained

3. How does your group compare with other similar groups on each of the following points?

	Better Than Most	About the Same as Most	Not as Good as Most	Not Ascertained
a. The way the members get along together				
b. The way the members stick together				
c. The way the members help each other on the job				

Source: Stanley Seashore, *Group Cohesiveness in the Industrial Work Group* (Ann Arbor, MI: Institute for Social Research, University of Michigan, 1954), 301.

GENERAL MEETING EVALUATION FORM

Circle the number that best reflects your evaluation of this meeting. Include comments for improvement beneath each question.

1. Most members participated appropriately.
    Yes   1   2   3   4   5   6   7   No
    Comments:

2. There was active listening by most members (paraphrasing, responding to points made, summarizing others' points, nonverbal feedback).
    Always   1   2   3   4   5   6   7   Never
    Comments:

3. Everyone was prepared for the meeting.
    Prepared 1   2   3   4   5   6   7   Unprepared
    Comments:

4. Discussion was focused and stayed on the topic or task.
    Always   1   2   3   4   5   6   7   Never
    Comments:

5. Members' responses were clear, brief, and terms were defined.
    Always   1   2   3   4   5   6   7   Never
    Comments:

6. The agenda was followed with efficiency.
    Always   1   2   3   4   5   6   7   Never
    Comments:

7. When evaluation or criticisms were offered, they were phrased constructively.
    Always   1   2   3   4   5   6   7   Never
    Comments:

8. There was an atmosphere of cooperation.
    Always   1   2   3   4   5   6   7   Never
    Comments:

9. Members were willing to offer opinions, ask questions, and contribute to discussion.
    Always   1   2   3   4   5   6   7   Never
    Comments:

10. Evaluation of opinions, ideas, proposals, and information was thorough and carefully done.
    Always   1   2   3   4   5   6   7   Never
    Comments:

11. Relationships among members appeared to be friendly and pleasant.
    Always   1   2   3   4   5   6   7   Never
    Comments:

12. Members volunteered to perform tasks and accept responsibility.
    Always   1   2   3   4   5   6   7   Never
    Comments:

13. The meeting room's environment was conducive to conducting business.
    Yes   1   2   3   4   5   6   7   No
    Comments:

Appendix D:
IAF Draft Statement of Values and Code of Ethics for Facilitators

The IAF Ethics and Values Think Tank (EVTT) has concluded its work in developing a Statement of Values and Ethics for Group Facilitators (the Code).

The following Draft Statement of Values and Code of Ethics (the Code) was adopted by the Association Coordinating Team (ACT) on May 21, 2002, and will be formally reviewed in two years.

The work of EVTT has taken place over two years (June 2000–May 2002) and has involved an estimated 150 people. An online group of 85 people exchanging more than 900 emails and engaged in thousands of thinking and discussion hours on the EVTT e-group. In addition 2 forums involving 40 people were held at IAF Conference 2001 at Minnesota. Workshops and discussions were also held at regional conferences and on regional e-groups.

The development of the Code has involved a wide diversity of views and the working through of different perspectives to achieve a consensus across regional and cultural boundaries. This has taken a considerable effort and is a major achievement.

The Code was adopted by ACT on May 21, 2002, and will be formally reviewed in two years. During the two years the Ethics and Values Think Tank will solicit feedback from IAF members and other stakeholders, and continue to provide a forum for discussion of pertinent issues and potential revisions. The Code should be made widely available and copies distributed to all IAF members.

The International Association of Facilitators Draft Statement of Values and Code of Ethics for Facilitators (Adopted May 21, 2002)

PREAMBLE

Facilitators are called upon to fill an impartial role in helping groups become more effective. We act as process guides to create a balance between participation and results.

We, the members of the International Association of Facilitators (IAF), believe that our profession gives us a unique opportunity to make a positive contribution to individuals, organizations, and society. Our effectiveness is based on our personal integrity and the trust developed between ourselves and those with whom we work. Therefore, we recognise the importance of defining and making known the values and ethical principles that guide our actions.

This Statement of Values and Code of Ethics recognizes the complexity of our roles, including the full spectrum of personal, professional and cultural diversity in the IAF membership and in the field of facilitation. Members of the International Association of Facilitators are committed to using these values and ethics to guide their professional practice. These principles are expressed in broad statements to guide ethical practice; they provide a framework and are not intended to dictate conduct for particular situations. Questions or advice about the application of these values and ethics may be addressed to the International Association of Facilitators.

STATEMENT OF VALUES

As group facilitators, we believe in the inherent value of the individual and the collective wisdom of the group. We strive to help the group make the best use of the contributions of each of its members. We set aside our personal opinions and support the group's right to make its own choices. We believe that collaborative and cooperative interaction builds consensus and produces meaningful outcomes. We value professional collaboration to improve our profession.

CODE OF ETHICS

1. Client Service

We are in service to our clients, using our group facilitation competencies to add value to their work.

Our clients include the groups we facilitate and those who contract with us on their behalf. We work closely with our clients to understand their expectations so that we provide the appropriate service, and that the group produces the desired outcomes. It is our responsibility to ensure that we are competent to handle the intervention. If the group decides it needs to go in a direction other than that originally intended by either the group or its representatives, our role is to help the group move forward, reconciling the original intent with the emergent direction.

2. Conflict of Interest

We openly acknowledge any potential conflict of interest.

Prior to agreeing to work with our clients, we discuss openly and honestly any possible conflict of interest, personal bias, prior knowledge of the organisation or any other matter which may be perceived as preventing us from working effectively with the interests of all group members. We do this so that, together, we may make an informed decision about proceeding and to prevent misunderstanding that could detract from the success or credibility of the clients or ourselves. We refrain from using our position to secure unfair or inappropriate privilege, gain, or benefit.

3. Group Autonomy

We respect the culture, rights, and autonomy of the group.

We seek the group's conscious agreement to the process and their commitment to participate. We do not impose anything that risks the welfare and dignity of the participants, the freedom of choice of the group, or the credibility of its work.

4. Processes, Methods, and Tools

We use processes, methods and tools responsibly.

In dialogue with the group or its representatives we design processes that will achieve the group's goals, and select and adapt the most appropriate methods and tools. We avoid using processes, methods or tools with which we are insufficiently skilled, or which are poorly matched to the needs of the group.

5. Respect, Safety, Equity, and Trust

We strive to engender an environment of respect and safety where all participants trust that they can speak freely and where individual boundaries are honoured. We use our skills, knowledge, tools, and wisdom to elicit and honour the perspectives of all.

We seek to have all relevant stakeholders represented and involved. We promote equitable relationships among the participants and facilitator and ensure that all participants have an opportunity to examine and share their thoughts and feelings. We use a variety of methods to enable the group to access the natural gifts, talents and life experiences of each member. We work in ways that honour the wholeness and self-expression of others, designing sessions that respect different styles of interaction. We understand that any action we take is an intervention that may affect the process.

6. Stewardship of Process

We practice stewardship of process and impartiality toward content.

While participants bring knowledge and expertise concerning the substance of their situation, we bring knowledge and expertise concerning the group interaction process. We are vigilant to minimize our influence on group outcomes. When we have content knowledge not otherwise available to the group, and that the group must have to be effective, we offer it after explaining our change in role.

7. Confidentiality

We maintain confidentiality of information.

We observe confidentiality of all client information. Therefore, we do not share information about a client within or outside of the client's organisation, nor do we report on group content, or the individual opinions or behaviour of members of the group without consent.

8. Professional Development

We are responsible for continuous improvement of our facilitation skills and knowledge.

We continuously learn and grow. We seek opportunities to improve our knowledge and facilitation skills to better assist groups in their work. We remain current in the field of facilitation through our practical group experiences and ongoing personal development. We offer our skills within a spirit of collaboration to develop our professional work practices.

IAF'S ETHICS AND VALUES THINK TANK

Rationale

IAF has moved forward in adopting a set of competencies and a certification program for the same. An important complement to competencies is a coherent set of values or ethical standards that guide the application of those competencies. A "code of profession ethics" or "statement of core values" or similar document (hereinafter referred to as "code") will further strengthen the credibility of group facilitation as a profession, enhance the professional identity of group facilitators, and avoid misconceptions of group facilitation by existing and potential customers.

Purpose

To create a "code of professional ethics," "statement of core values" or similar document that can be formally adopted by the IAF and made available for adoption by individual members. Members may then indicate to existing and potential customers that they have agreed to adhere to the code and may provide the customer with a copy of it.

Major Tasks

- Develop a two-year plan for creating and implementing a code.

- Gather and examine similar documents from other professional organizations.

- Develop among Think Tank members a draft document. Consult with professional ethicists and other professional societies as needed.

- Draft a document for review by ACT.

- Revise and make available a draft to all members.

- Conduct a Think Tank session at IAF Conference 2001.

- Revise and recirculate a draft to ACT and make available to all members.

- Develop training materials.

- At IAF 2002 present code to ACT (and perhaps to general membership) for formal adoption.

- Test our training materials at Think Tank session at IAF 2002.

- Finalize training materials and make available to IAF members.

Anyone interested in participating in the continuing development of the Statement of Values and Code of Ethics for Group Facilitators should join the Ethics and Values Think Tank, http://groups.yahoo.com/group/EVTT.

Bibliography

ARTICLES

Baker, Deborah C. "A Qualitative and Quantitative Analysis of Verbal Style and the Elimination of Potential Leaders in Small Groups." *Communication Quarterly* 39 (Winter 1990): 13–26.

Barge, J. Kevin, and Randy Y. Hirokawa. "Toward a Communication Competency of Group Leadership." *Small Group Behavior* 20 (1989): 167–189.

Benne, Kenneth D., and Paul Sheats. "Functional Roles of Group Members." *Journal of Social Issues* 4 (Spring 1948): 41–49.

Broome, Benjamin J., and Luann Fulbright. "A Multistage Influence Model of Barriers to Group Problem Solving: A Participant-Generated Agenda for Small Group Research." *Small Group Research* 26 (February 1995): 25–55.

Fisher, B. Aubrey. "Leadership as Medium: Treating Complexity in Group Communication Research." *Small Group Behavior* 16 (1985): 167–196.

Geier, John C. "A Trait Approach to the Study of Leadership in Small Groups." *Journal of Communication* 17 (1967): 316–323.

Gouran, Dennis S. "The Watergate Cover-up: Its Dynamics and Its Implications." *Communication Monographs* 43 (1976): 176–186.

Hirokawa, Randy Y., and Dierdre D. Johnston. "Toward a General Theory of Decision-making: Development of an Integrated Model." *Small Group Behavior* 20 (November 1989): 500–523.

International Association of Facilitators. "The International Association of Facilitators Draft Statement of Values and Code of Ethics for Facilitators." IAF Web site, http://www.iaf-world.org/iafethicsTT.htm.

Jehn, K.A. "A Multimethod Examination of the Benefits and Determinants of Intragroup Conflict." *Administrative Science Quarterly* 40 (1995): 256–282.

Katzenbach, Jon R., and Douglas K. Smith. "The Discipline of Teams." *Harvard Business Review* (March–April 1993): 111–120.

Kuhn, T., and M.S. Poole. "Do Conflict Management Styles Affect Group Decision Making? Evidence from a Longitudinal Field Study." *Human Communication Research* 4 (October 2000): 558–590.

Kurke, L.B., and H.E. Aldrich. "Mintzberg Was Right! A Replication and Extension of the Nature of Managerial Work." *Management Science* 29.8 (1979): 975–984.

McLeod, P.L., and J.K. Liker. "Electronic Meeting Systems: Evidence from a Low Structure Environment." *Information Systems Research* 3 (1992): 195–223.

Moreland, Richard, and John Levine. "Socialization in Small Groups: Temporal Changes in Individual Group Relations." *Advances in Experimental Social Psychology* 15 (1982): 137–193.

Moser, M. "Ethical Conflict at Work." *Journal of Business Ethics* 7 (1988): 381–387.

Oshagbemi, Titus. "Management Development and Managers' Use of Their Time." *Journal of Management Development* 14.8 (1995): 7.

Pelled, L.H., K.M. Eisenhardt, and K.R. Xin. "Exploring the Black Box: An Analysis of Work Group Diversity, Conflict, and Performance." *Administrative Science Quarterly* 44 (1999): 1–28.

Posner, B.Z., and W.H. Schmidt. "Values and the American Manager." *California Management Review* 26 (1984): 202–216.

Salazar, Abran J. "Understanding the Synergistic Effects of Communication in Small Groups: Making the Most Out of Group Member Abilities." *Small Group Research* 26 (May 1995): 169–199.

Schacter, Stanley. "Deviation, Rejection and Communication." *Journal of Abnormal and Social Psychology* 46 (1951): 190–207.

Schanck, Robert L. "A Study of a Community and Its Groups and Institutions Conceived of as Behaviors of Individuals." *Psychological Monographs* 43 (1932): 195.

Scheffler, A.E. "Quasi-Courtship Behavior in Psychotherapy." *Psychiatry* 28 (1965): 245–256.

Sherif, Muzafer, B. Jack White, and O.J. Harvey. "Status in Experimentally Produced Groups." *American Journal of Sociology* 60 (1955): 370–379.

Torrance, E. Paul. "Some Consequences of Power Differences on Decision Making in Permanent and Temporary Three-Man Groups." *Research Studies Washington State College* 22 (1954): 130–140.

BOOKS

Ausubel, Nathan, ed. *A Treasury of Jewish Folklore: Stories, Traditions, Legends, Humor, Wisdom and Folk Songs of the Jewish People*. New York: Crown, 1948.

Bales, Robert F., and Edgar F. Borgatta. "Size of a Group as a Factor in the Interaction Profile." In *Small Groups: Studies in Social Interaction*, ed. Paul A. Hare, Edgar F. Borgatta, and Robert F. Bales. New York: Knopf, 1965.

Beebe, Steven A., and John T. Masterson. *Communicating in Small Groups: Principles and Practices*, 5th ed. New York: Longman, 1997.

Block, Peter. *Flawless Consulting: A Guide to Getting Your Expertise Used*. San Diego, CA: University Associates, 1981.

Bormann, Ernest G. *Small Group Discussion: Theory and Practice*, 3rd ed. New York: Harper & Row, 1990.

Burgoon, Judee K., and Thomas Saine. *The Unknown Dialogue: An Introduction to Nonverbal Communication*. Boston: Houghton Mifflin, 1978.

Carpenter, Edmund, and Marshall McLuhan, eds. *Explorations in Communication*. Boston: Beacon Press, 1960.

Choran, I. "The Manager of a Small Company." Master's thesis, McGill University, Montreal, 1976. Referenced in Morgan W. McCall and Michael M. Lombardo, "Looking Glass Inc.: The First Three Years." *Technical Report* 13. Greensboro, NC: Center for Creative Leadership, 1979.

Conrad, Charles. *Strategic Organizational Communication: Toward the Twenty-First Century*, 3rd ed. Fort Worth, TX: Harcourt Brace College Publishers, 1994.

Davis, Brian, L., Carol J. Skube, Lowell W. Hellervik, Susan H. Gebelein, and James L. Sheard. *The Successful Manager's Handbook: Development Suggestions for Today's Managers*. Minneapolis, MN: Personnel Decisions, Inc., 1992.

Drucker, Peter F. *People and Performance: The Best of Peter Drucker on Management*. London: Heinemann, 1977.

Eccles, Robert G., and Nitin Nohria. 1992. *Beyond the Hype: Rediscovering the Essence of Management*. Boston: Harvard Business School Press, 1992.

Fiedler, Fred E. *A Theory of Leadership Effectiveness*. New York: McGraw-Hill, 1967.

Folger, Joseph P., Marshall Scott Poole, and Randall K. Stutman. *Working Through Conflict: Strategies for Relationships, Groups, and Organizations*, 3rd ed. New York: HarperCollins, 1997.

Follett, Mary Parker. *The New State*. New York: Longman, Green & Co., 1918.

Funk & Wagnalls. *New Comprehensive International Dictionary of the English Language*. Newark, NJ: Publishers International Press, 1982.

Galanes, Gloria J., and John K. Brilhart. *Communicating in Groups: Applications and Skills*, 3rd ed. Madison, WI: Brown and Benchmark Publishers, 1997.

Hall, Calvin S., and Gardner Lindzey. *Theories of Personality*, 3rd ed. New York: John Wiley & Sons, 1978.

Hall, Edward T. *The Hidden Dimension*. Garden City, NY: Anchor, 1969.

Heimer, Carol. "Doing Your Job and Helping Your Friends: Universalistic Norms about Particular Others in Networks." In *Networks and Organizations: Structure, Form and Action*, ed. Nitin Nohria and Robert G. Eccles. Boston: Harvard Business School Press, 1992, 247–265.

Homans, George C. *Social Behavior: Its Elementary Forms*, 2nd ed. New York: Harcourt, Brace, Jovanovich, 1974.

Ishikawa, Kaoru. *What Is Total Quality Control?* Englewood Cliffs, NJ: Prentice Hall, 1985.

Kawakita, Jiro. *KJ Method: A Scientific Approach to Problem Solving*. Tokyo: Kawakita Research Institute, 1975.

Kendon, Adam. "Gesticulation and Speech: Two Aspects of the Process of Utterance." In *The Relationship of Verbal and Nonverbal Communication*, ed. Mary Ritchie Key. The Hague: Mouton, 1980, 207–227.

Kendon, Adam. "How Gestures Can Become Like Words." In *Cross-Cultural Perspectives in Nonverbal Communication*, ed. Fernando Poyatos. Toronto: Hogrefe, 1997. Also "Gesture" in *Annual Review of Anthropology* 26: 109–128.

Kreps, Gary L. *Organizational Communication: Theory and Practice*. New York: Longman, 1986.

Lawrence, Peter. *Management in Action*. London: Routledge and Kegan Paul, 1984.

Likert, Rensis. *New Patterns of Management*, ed. Arthur P. Brief. New York: Garland Publishing, 1987.

Marx, Karl. *The Communist Manifesto*. In *The Marx-Engels Reader*, ed. Robert C. Tucker. New York: W.W. Norton, 1972.

McGregor, Douglas. *The Human Side of Enterprise*, rev. ed. New York: McGraw-Hill/Irwin, 1985.

Milgram, Stanley. *Obedience to Authority*. New York: Harper Colophon Books, 1969.

Mintzberg, Henry. *The Nature of Managerial Work*. New York: Harper & Row, 1973.

Parker, Glenn M. *Parker Team Player Survey*. Palo Alto, CA: Consulting Psychologists Press, 1991.

Seashore, Stanley. *Group Cohesiveness in the Industrial Work Group.* Ann Arbor, MI: Institute for Social Research, University of Michigan, 1954.

Toffler, Barbara Ley. *Tough Choices: Managers Talk Ethics.* New York: John Wiley, 1986.

Weik, Karl. *The Social Psychology of Organizing,* 2nd ed. Reading, MA: Addison-Wesley, 1979.

Weisbord, Marvin R. *Productive Workplaces: Organizing and Managing for Dignity, Meaning, and Community.* San Francisco: Jossey-Bass, 1989.

Index

About the Author

MARVIN R. GOTTLIEB is President of the Communication Project, Inc. His worldwide consulting practice in management training and development has included work for American Express, A.T. Kearney, Bankers Trust, Ernst & Young, Ogilvy & Mather, E.D.S., Instinet, The Prudential, and UBS Paine Webber. An Associate Professor of Communication at Lehman College, City University of New York for 30 years, he has been in the forefront of computer-based distance learning instructional design for proprietary networks and the Internet.